PAWS for FRIENDSHIP

The journey of Jennie - a little Great Dane

By Jan Schmidt
President of Paws for Friendship Inc.

authorHOUSE

AuthorHouse™
1663 Liberty Drive
Bloomington, IN 47403
www.authorhouse.com
Phone: 833-262-8899

Published by AuthorHouse 04/10/2023

ISBN: 979-8-8230-0135-9 (sc)
ISBN: 979-8-8230-0136-6 (e)

Print information available on the last page.

This book is printed on acid-free paper.

PAWS for FRIENDSHIP

*The story of Jennie, helping
those in need - one paw at a time*

By: Jan Schmidt
President of Paws for Friendship Inc.

Editor: Dottie Stanfill

"Never forget we are celebrating 30 years because of you sharing your little angels. There will never be a way to thank you as much as you need to be thanked. We are sincerely grateful to you. You make us the group we are today, and we can't begin to thank you enough. Extra hugs to all our well adored babies."

Jan Schmidt

Dedication

*This book is dedicated to Jennie, a little Great Dane,
and all the animals that have touched the lives
of those in need because of her legacy.*

CONTENTS

Part III
All about PAWS

FROM THE EDITOR

As the 30th anniversary of the founding of Paws for Friendship was approaching, I spoke to Jan Schmidt, the President, about the possibility of writing a book to commemorate the event. Jan's reaction was basically that she would not know where to start, that she felt she was not qualified for such a task, but that she LOVED the idea. Would I be able to help her put it together? Could we make it happen?

Having been a member of Paws for ten years, and being aware of the myriad lives that have been touched by people and pets who belong to this organization, I wanted to do whatever I could to make the book a reality. So I jumped on board, started looking for a publisher, began gathering stories, and this is the culmination of those efforts.

The writing of this book would not have been possible without that little Great Dane, Jennie, without Jan's vision 30 years ago, without the contributions of numerous members, and without the submission of their personal photographs. I must note here that Jan wants it to be perfectly clear that she is not the "founder" of Paws - Jennie is. In Jan's words, "I'm not the Founder, just the president. Dottie, I swear to you, I literally turned around to run away and she pulled me into the facility. I give myself **no** credit, I just did the paperwork and continue to this day, but she knew, well before I did, we were supposed to be there. You can put down that I was her 'designated driver'."

It has been my privilege and honor to help with this 30th anniversary gift to the world. Our hope is that, by reading about Jennie and Paws for Friendship, anyone who has ever had a desire to share the love and comfort of a precious pet will see this as an open door to the possibilities that exist. Helping those in need – whether at an assisted living facility, a library, a hospital, or during an unexpected tragedy – is a gift that will not only change *your* life by sharing, but will leave a lasting impact on *every life* you and your pet touch.

Dottie Stanfill, Editor and
Member - Paws for Friendship Inc.
Terre Haute, Indiana

SPECIAL THANKS

A special thank you goes to Kimberly Hicks, Paws member from Nebraska, who created and designed the 30-year patch for Paws for Friendship featured on the cover of the book.

A note of gratitude goes to Doris Parlette, from Bloomington, Indiana, a friend and fellow dog lover, who volunteered to help with the editing and proofreading of the book.

Thank you, also, to Ron Lesniak, a Paws member from Connecticut, who is the current registrar for Paws for Friendship, Inc. and who organized the information about facilities and people served, the cities and states that are represented, and the countless volunteer hours amassed.

And our gratitude goes out to the various members who shared pictures and who submitted personal stories of how their pets have helped those in need through the years.

Finally, thank you to Jennie, that little Great Dane, who has crossed over the Rainbow Bridge. This book, her legacy, the thousands of lives touched - none of it would be possible without her. Rest in peace, dear founder.

FROM THE AUTHOR

After all my adventures of 69 years, writing my biography is not easy. This book is not about me. It's about an angel who started the journey, and I hope as you read, you will see and sense the magnitude of what Jennie started 30 years ago.

I had a wonderful childhood, raised by loving parents. We certainly had our share of ups and downs, but overall, my childhood was great. The foundation I stand on today is because of my parents. When I hear stories of childhood abuse many have lived through, I cannot relate. I will listen and sympathize, but I just can't relate.

I have tried to live my life the best way I could - respecting those who returned the respect and reacting to those who did not. The latter group is no longer in my life, and I am better for it. One inherits many qualities from their parents. Love for animals was the best inheritance my parents could have given me. This has followed me throughout my life, and as the days pass, this has only increased ten-fold.

I am a homebody. I enjoy watching old movies, am sentimental to a fault (I'm told), love reading books, spending time with friends, and traveling, when possible, to enjoy new adventures. My adventures used to include camping well above the timberline, cooking on an open campfire, and praying the tent I set up would endure the storms that would suddenly appear. Those were the days – memories I will always hold close. I love the mountains, as they have always held a peace and contentment for me. My adventures now are completely different, but are just as memorable.

To describe how my life changed to what it is today involves heartbreak and believing against all odds that miracles do happen. One happened to me that literally saved my life. Her name was Jennie, and I will always believe divine intervention played a big part. When my life seemed at its darkest, a ray of sunshine appeared that would forever alter my path and, I am extremely proud to say, touched thousands of lives. This book is dedicated to that little Great Dane who had been rescued from an abusive home. When I first met her, I knew she needed me as much as I needed her. I was wrong. I needed her more and was blessed to share 11 ½ years with this angel. Not a day passes that I don't miss her. My life was given a gift from God at the darkest time in my life, and Jennie was the one who taught me about living every day with gratitude.

Thirty years later I am forever following her path and will until I no longer draw a breath. Many chose to turn back their "odometer", but not me. I want everyone to know I've traveled a long way and many of the roads were not paved. Jennie knew our path of travel before I did, and I am blessed because of her guidance.

Life grants us the opportunity to write our own destiny. Our fate is not a matter of chance; it is how we decide to spend our lives. Let us choose to give our lives to something that will outlast us. "Time to Live" is the title of a beautiful framed print in my office. The picture is a gorgeous mountain scene where your thoughts can rest and just drift away to wonderful memories of days gone by. The phrase says it all, and I find it especially true for me.

To everyone who has faithfully followed us through the years, thank you. To my dear friends who have never questioned my path of travel, thank you. Many did not understand the path I chose but you are still there, and I thank you. To all our members who have unconditionally shared their precious angels through the years, thank you. To say I am grateful to know them cannot scratch the surface of how I feel. Being a volunteer is the most wonderful way a person can spend their life. Teamed with a loving, caring, and faithful four-legged friend, touching lives and bringing smiles to those who are often forgotten – well, there is nothing more noble. My life has been filled with blessings, and I count you among them. I will forever be grateful that you walked with Jennie and me.

Jan Schmidt,
President, Paws for Friendship Inc.
Tampa, Florida

PART I

JENNIE'S STORY

This is a story of a little Great Dane puppy who rescued a lost soul. Life has a way of making miracles appear when you least expect one. It is always an adventure to find that, even though you may think you are lost, you are right where you need to be. This is the story of a miracle, and her name was Jennie.

When you suffer a personal loss, such as a parent, your heart feels as if it will never heal. You don't think life will ever make sense again, and you start believing that is now your new life. The next steps you take will shape your life. Was I aware this personal loss of Mom would set me on a new path? No, I was not. Jennie showed me that path.

GROWING UP IN OZ

My parents and I were always close; my friends were their friends, and it seemed our house was always the place to be. That was my childhood: no secrets, no disrespect, no sneaking out in the middle of the night to go somewhere I didn't really want to go anyway. I was very spoiled and loved spending time at home. I knew nothing of abuse, neglect, or going without food and comfort. Back in the day, those stories of neglect and abuse were rarely heard. They certainly were not part of *my* life.

I had always loved animals. My parents were both raised on farms, so loving animals was natural to me. I grew up around dogs of all sizes, birds, and tropical fish. Once, Dad brought home a stray dog that was only staying "temporarily." I learned at an early age his version of "temporarily" was completely different from that of anyone else I knew. "Temporarily" meant until they passed away naturally. Mom always welcomed each animal with open arms. She warned me, "Your father thinks he is being clever with his 'temporarily' but I learned years ago what his definition was." To say it simply, I thought I lived my childhood in the land of Oz.

I had always loved horses, and any opportunity to ride one was a dream come true. When I turned 13 my parents bought me my first horse, Penni. They had purchased an acreage, and I cannot remember a day I didn't have a smile on my face when I was out there. Penni and I traveled the area as if we were scouting new territories. My parents were convinced I would soon "outgrow" horses for boys and cars. That is not exactly how things turned out. In fact, they bought a bigger acreage to build their dream home. Dad always promised Mom that he would build her a new house. With him as the contractor, a new home was built.

Now, after seven horses and multiple chickens, ducks, geese, turkeys, peacocks, chukars, rabbits, goats, one lamb, and a miniature Sicilian donkey, they had given up hope on the boys and cars idea. Dad was self-employed, and Mom was the bookkeeper. To me, they defined what love was all about. I could not imagine one without the other. With each step in building their dream home, you could tell they were both so excited. I just knew life couldn't get any better.

LIFE BRINGS CHANGE

You can imagine what I felt when Dad told me one evening, "When something happens to me, you will have to take care of your mom." I immediately said, "Why are you asking? Why are you even telling me this?" I will never forget the look on his face. He said, "I can't stay forever, so promise you will take care of your mom." Of course, I promised, all the while wondering why he asked. It was never mentioned again.

When their dream home was almost completed, Dad had a heart attack, and was admitted to the hospital. Now, to me, he was invincible, so the heart attack was a complete shock. The dream house was so close to being finished! How dare he suffer a heart attack! All the while, his doctors kept Mom informed. I suddenly saw a change in her. She seemed so fragile, so frightened, so lost.

We were told that, when he would be released, he should not have any stairs to climb while getting better. That was just the direction we needed, and it could easily be done. Over a short period of time, we had everything moved from the only home I had ever known to their new dream house. We made sure everything would be perfect when he came home. He had no idea we had done this. On the Fourth of July, we were visiting Dad early afternoon, and had planned on watching the fireworks that evening from his hospital room. Suddenly, he began to have breathing problems. The nurses and doctors rushed in while we leaned against the walls waiting for them to help him. Mom was talking to him, and I couldn't find any words, so I stood alongside her. I watched Dad pass away and I saw Mom shattered.

Later we left and headed home, to their dream home. She told me she was not ready to go there right then, so we drove around in silence. When she said, "Let's go home," we did. That evening she stared out the windows overlooking the back yard. Nothing was said. The morning came only too soon, and I had no idea how I could help her. Even our dogs were careful about everything, as if they knew. I asked her if she wanted to go out and feed the outside animals, and she shook her head. It seemed the better part of her had gone with him.

Months passed slowly, and she found no comfort in being in their dream home without him. It was like she had made her mind up to just give up and exist. She gave me power of attorney to close the business down and handle some things. And all the while, I watched her give up a little more each day. I remembered what Dad had asked me, and I somehow managed to step up for him.

More time passed, and she suffered three strokes. There was nothing to console her; she had given up. Never in my lifetime had I visited a rehab center or nursing home. All too soon I became a seasoned visitor. Because of her refusal to try, her movements were restricted to a wheelchair. Soon, circulation was the problem. Little did I know what was to be the outcome. We hired extra healthcare so that, when I went to work, she was never alone. Our neighbors were angels, helping any way they could, especially with the animals. Thank God I did not have to worry about them! After learning that one of her legs had to be amputated because there was no circulation, she began to understand the reality of the situation. I would like to say she accepted it, but she refused to have surgery.

In the hospital, she began to argue with me. Now, to say I loved Mom and Dad would be the understatement of the year, but Mom started to blame me for having the surgery. She was convinced I was part of this "group" that said her leg must come off. As I tried to explain, she got louder, and I got louder, and a nurse came in to see what she could do. I said, "Nothing! She is stubborn and refuses to have the surgery!" The discussion finally ended at 4:30 AM, and she was to have surgery first thing that morning. She told me, "Sign the Consent Form so if I die, it will be on your head!" She said I was a lousy daughter and she hoped I was happy forcing her to lose a leg. All I kept hearing was what Dad told me, and I had very broad shoulders.

She came through surgery fine and cried when she saw me, telling me she was glad I was there. I told her there was nowhere in the world I would rather be. From July 4, 1981, when Dad passed away, to that moment, I had known everything my Mom did. She loved Kenny Rogers, and when we heard he was going to be in concert an hour away, we went. When she wanted her hair done each Thursday, we went, just as she always did. Pretty much nothing stopped us. She began to enjoy seeing the animals, cooking out, enjoying time spent with neighbors and friends. This new life was welcomed after years of sadness.

When we learned that her other leg had to be removed, we went through the arguing phase again. She fired me as her daughter, and rehired me hours later, but once again, surgery was to be done.

During rehab at a care center, I learned how many people sit and wait in their wheelchairs for a visitor. Too often no visitor ever showed, which baffled me. I went at any hour she called and needed something. I even received calls at my job concerning it was her time to bring cookies to Bingo! My boss was beyond understanding, and my friends were always there when I needed them. As I wrote down exactly what kind of cookie to bring and how many, I thought this was great! She was finally comfortable playing Bingo and had a new circle of friends. I thought, who knows when the next adventure will come! All I knew was that I had to be ready when it did.

She came back home, and a hospital bed was now in the living room so she could look out the floor to ceiling windows. One day she was really depressed, and I asked what I could do. She asked how Jake was (Jake was our little Sicilian donkey). I said he...well, everyone was great. She continued to stare out the front windows, as if she were waiting for someone. I said I will be right back, so don't go anywhere. She laughed like she hadn't in quite a while. It sounded like a choir to me.

I walked Jake into the living room to surprise her, and he was such a clown anyway, of course, he showed her how he could smile, and he started braying loudly. That scared the dogs out of the living room, but he just kept it up. We both laughed, and he kept nudging her to pet him, and she did gladly. After a while, and many caregivers later, she needed more care--almost acute care. After going into so many care facilities after her surgeries, it seemed nothing had changed. Many residents still sat and waited for any kindness, even from a stranger. Mom settled into a facility she preferred, and after a while she was playing games, visiting with others, and it seemed she was going to be ok.

Having an incredibly understanding boss, I was able to take things she needed to her during the day. The request list always included food of some type for herself and her tablemates. Soon, I was visiting with everyone I had passed while going to visit her. Stories explaining why their family was "running late" to see them were beginning to be the norm. When I talked to Mom about it, she just said their families dumped most of them and walked away. I could never figure out how anyone could do that.

For seven years I always knew where Mom was and what she was doing. Her schedule was part of my life. No matter what the strokes did, she was always my mom, my best friend. I was fired when she disagreed with me, rehired later, and then, for some reason I could not fathom, she had gotten sick. Regardless of amputated legs and a left side pretty much paralyzed, she was still my mom.

In the hospital, after the tests were run, results seemed to take forever. I was grateful she liked all her doctors. I was finally told what was happening. She was not told anything right away and I was grateful for that. In the hallway, it was explained to me as simply as possible. This was supposed to give me time "to be prepared to lose her." How in God's name was I supposed to do that? One of her doctors I greatly admired--Mom also fired and rehired him, too, when he didn't agree with her. We had a bond. He tried to explain things to me, and I wanted to be an adult and listen and understand, but this was MY mom. I told him for seven years I knew where she was and what she was doing; her schedule was my schedule for seven years since we lost Dad. He tried and tried to be rational with me, and finally saw he was getting nowhere.

He smiled and hugged me. He knew I understood and was trying to accept what he had said. I asked one thing from him, and he smiled and hugged me even tighter. I saw him every day he came to check on her, and she hadn't fired him in a while, so we were making progress. I went off to work as I always did, knowing she was well taken care of. I told him to let me know when I should *not* leave the hospital. He nodded, hugged me again, and went on to see his other patients.

On February 20, 1988, as I was talking to Mom about what the weather was supposed to do, he came in to visit her. She smiled and told him, "The 'kid' is here again, missing work again to see me." He said, "Well, I think she just doesn't trust your doctors, so she comes all the time to see for herself how you are doing." That brought a big smile from her. He asked her if she needed anything, and she pointed at me and said just her. I smiled and got up and stepped out of her room to cry.

He came out and hugged me and whispered, "Don't leave." Back in her room I went, wiping away any sign of crying, and we talked about the animals and was I taking care of them and myself. I said, "Always." Then she looked at me and said she could never say goodbye to me. I said we won't say goodbye, there was no reason to say goodbye. Earlier, I had called my boss and told him I would not be in. I had given him a list of friends to notify in case anything happened, and he had called them. I didn't even realize some of my friends were in the room. I told Mom I loved her, and she said, "I love you too, but I can't say goodbye to you." She looked right into my eyes and smiled and then closed her eyes. It was not real to me; nobody could console me. We left the room and after the nurse told me I could go back in, I did. She had brushed Mom's hair and arranged the pillows, so it appeared she was sleeping.

I told her I knew Dad was there, and they would never be separated again. She was finally, after seven years without Dad, where she wanted to be. I told her she would never want for anything ever again, and she could finally rest. I took her personal belongings and rolled out the wheelchair she had used since the strokes. No words spoken helped; nothing seemed to matter anymore. I loaded her wheelchair into the back of my truck, put her personal belongings on the front seat by me, and drove back home. I had animals to feed and calls to make. I had a routine I had to continue. By now a friend had called the neighbors, and they had already fed my animals. Some stopped by to see what else they could do. I thanked them and hugged them until it seemed my tears would never stop.

Planning her funeral was something I had to get through. I kept hearing what Dad had told me years ago. When he was gone, I had promised him I would take care of Mom, and I had done the best I could. The funeral home was so crowded that many were waiting outside to pay their respects. Beautiful flowers filled the chapel, friends hugged me, neighbors hugged me, and everyone offered to help me any way they could.

Months seemed to drag by, and I had lost my compass to my life. For seven years I had known where she was and what she was doing. Each Thursday, she had a hair appointment. With each day that passed, it slowly began to sink in that she was really gone. With what I thought was my only hope to find sense again in the world, I locked my horses in the corral, so they were safe. I walked to the top of the acreage my parents bought for their dream home, and just lay down in the grass. My goal was to end my life because it didn't seem to matter to me anymore. I had my revolver all loaded and ready; I just had to make sure the time was right.

Several hours later I woke to find all my horses standing over me just looking at me. I could not believe they had walked up the hill and I had heard nothing. I had safely locked them in the corral so they would not be anywhere near me when I took my life. This was impossible! They were all just standing there, as if wondering what I was doing. We all walked slowly back to the barn. Everyone stayed in step with me; slowly down the hill we went. The gate to the corral was wide open. I decided I was supposed to be here, so I had better hope and pray for a path to continue.

SAVED BY AN ANGEL

In early fall of that year, I was told about a six-month-old Great Dane puppy that was to be destroyed. The puppy was supposedly "mean and out of control," and the owner was going to put her down. Would I go look and see what I thought? I arrived to find a Great Dane in the back yard staying as far away from me as possible. She was on the ground, shaking. She had cuts on her left paw, untreated. She looked as if she had been abused and she stared right at me. I wondered who could possibly do this to her! As I sat down on the ground, she came to me, crawling slowly with great caution. She had no idea if I would continue the abuse, yet she came to me.

I reached out to her, and she bowed her head as if she expected to be beaten. Her eyes told me she needed love and kindness and asked if I was "the one" to give it to her. What she didn't know was that divine intervention brought us together. I needed her far more than she ever needed me. We went home together, and I knew she had saved my life. The least I could do for her was to love her beyond the definition of the word. For eleven and a half years she wanted for nothing. I learned firsthand all about blessings and how they arrived in different ways. The day we met was also Mom's birthday, so I knew divine intervention brought us together. She was my angel.

We began a period of trust that would last to this very day in my heart. She had never had any treats, babies to cuddle, good quality food, grooming or hugs. She learned quickly how wonderful these were. They became part of her life, and she began to teach me all about fitting in to a world I had given up on. I was a piece of clay at that time, and she molded me into the person I thought I had lost. Through loving her I found me, and she knew it. They say God never closes a door without opening a window. He certainly opened a window for me, and her name was now Jennie. I renamed her because I wanted all the evil done to her erased with the name she had. She seemed fine with the new name, so another step ahead was taken. Since no record of her birthday was given to me, I chose Thanksgiving Day, and she seemed fine with that as well.

I knew there was just something about her. She was young, yet an "old soul." When I called her, and she looked at me, it was like she was looking into my soul. I may have put several barriers up with certain people so they would not know how badly I was feeling, both physically and emotionally. I was still fragile. Jennie saw through all that and I knew every fiber of my being was safe with her. She went through many changes; she was able to be a silly puppy and then a dog with such grace it amazed me. She had never known the puppy stage without being punished for it. Somehow, she knew nobody would ever hurt her again. The trust between us was secure and unbreakable.

I noticed her gentleness coming through. She was incredibly welcoming to anyone new. She just seemed to know nobody would ever raise a hand to hurt her again. Jennie greeted everyone as if they were long lost friends. My last thought was to return to any care centers after Mom passed away; it was the furthest thing from my mind, or so I thought. But filtering through my mind, while watching this dog embrace life, were the faces of those in the facilities, waiting for a visitor. I knew Jennie had saved my life but could, or would she have anything "extra" to give? She finally knew what treats were, and she had toy babies to cuddle and good food to enjoy. She had put on weight, and the scars were still there, but all the open cuts had healed from medication. Her coat was beautiful, and her eyes were finally bright and full of life. People saw a gentleness in her, as I did. Even after all the abuse, she forgave all of it; she was finally able to be herself. Even I was unaware of what lay ahead. I had been raised with dogs all my life, and with an assortment of animals through my years. I had loved them all with all my heart. My parents shared their love for animals with me. Jennie was different. She was like a person in a dog suit. I couldn't explain it if I wanted to. It was just a fact.

More and more, I thought about those residents who waited patiently for someone who never would arrive--a family member, a former neighbor, someone to brighten their day. Jennie and I took some obedience classes, more for me than her. I fell short on the discipline scale. It was quite simple from the start. Whatever she wanted, she got, often with multiple choices. We went several places she could go to shop for treats, etc. and enjoyed quiet times just as much. Every time we would be in public, people were drawn to her. Her size was impressive (she was over 6' 2" when she stood on her back legs), and she was gorgeous to look at.

The more I watched her, I would drift back to all those people waiting for any kindness. Was she capable of bringing her heart into those facilities? The more I watched her grow, the more convinced I was she could make a difference. Her biggest obstacle was me, and I believe she already knew that. All the while I thought I was training her and learning about her, she was miles ahead of me. She was working on *me*.

A NEW PATH COMING INTO VIEW

After five years of trusting each other, learning just when it was "time" for another treat, and finding out that life was wonderful, we drove to a care center. It was one Mom had rehab in after her surgery. It was not a special day, no holiday or anything. It was the first facility in which I had seen so many lonely faces. Memories of all those waiting for someone to visit, to show someone cared, came flooding back. I wanted to share this magnificent animal that had absolutely saved my life.

On the drive to the care center, I was talking to Jenny a million words a minute, and she was listening to every word. I could see it in her eyes. She could always look into my soul. We approached this black mat that would open the first door that led to the second door, and then we would be in. It looked very simple: just one black mat and we would be inside. Where we would go from there was easy. Hallways were left and right that would lead to many lonely people. I began to wonder if I would recognize anyone who had been there when Mom was. I was hoping not, because I wasn't prepared for that.

I suddenly felt a wave of terror and knew I could not do this-- after all those years and all those lonesome faces. I began to turn away just inches from that first mat and headed towards the van. I am far from a small person. I could throw bales of hay into a hayloft without giving another thought, beyond the 40th bale. I could move around

13

50-gallon drums full of grain for my horses without a thought. You can get the idea: helpless I was not. Suddenly, Jennie pulled me back around and literally forced me into this place. In a matter of seconds, I was powerless to this Great Dane who knew before I did that we were supposed to be there. After we were inside, she went over and put her head in this elderly lady's lap as if to say, "I'm here for you," and she looked at me as if to say, "Be my voice and I will be your strength." I did, and she was. So, you see … I wanted to run away; she *knew* we had to stay.

These are the facts of the beginning of Paws for Friendship, Incorporated. Had it not been for her, we never would have made that first visit. I would always remember those faces in the care centers as just a sad period in my life. Jennie defined my life; she gave it purpose. Her legacy is mine forever. She touched more lives than can ever be counted and took me along for the ride. She was my life's miracle.

AND SO IT BEGINS

How does one start an organization? That was the million-dollar question. The facts were scary. Paperwork I'd had no experience with soon became an obsession. I did not possess *any* computer skills. Now it became obvious I had to buy one, learn to use it and learn what "details" were really all about. To this day, I rue the start button on the computer. I believe it knows my skills are far from "perfected" when it comes to anything technical.

Another blessing entered my life in the form of a very understanding attorney who helped pave the way. He made sure all my Ts were crossed and my Is dotted. He offered suggestions, but he also criticized my decision to take my life savings and invest in complete strangers. By this time, we had become friends, and he felt comfortable, as I did, in asking him questions about starting this group of volunteers. In a new "language," foreign to me, he explained that I was investing in strangers who could join on a Monday; then, get upset with me for whatever reason and leave on a Thursday. But he also understood that I would still stand there believing I would find people who believed as I did. I will never forget the wisdom he gave me; it rings true to this day. He told me, "You are one of the few I have ever met that can take a direct hit and keep on going." I kept reminding him that making visits to care centers with a pet can change lives. Turns out, that was a fact. They could and did change many lives. Twenty-eight years later, they are still changing lives and making a difference.

He mentioned I could buy a vacation home, and travel when and where I wanted to go. I had a good job and could enjoy my money, visit new places, enjoy life, and just relax. The words really did make sense, to everyone else but me. This man even went as far as to say, "I think you are crazy to do this." I listened and did my usual nod that I really was listening to him. Occasionally, "the nod" is still used to appease someone. Most of the time it does work, unless that person knows me very well. I was now legally responsible for an organization whose foundation was wrapped around this little Great Dane named Jennie. If you ever want an experiment in how to start a volunteer organization, just ask me.

I have enjoyed the journey, once several stopped calling me crazy, insane, obsessed, etc. I could not argue with them, especially when donations were few and far between. When our organization could not pay the operating expenses, I did. Yes, it was as simple and complicated as that. I justified not buying that new vehicle, and I could always take *that* trip. There was no sense of urgency to do anything but protect our group that Jennie's courage, compassion, and love started. I was the "official" paper pusher; she was the heart and soul. She is still today the heart and soul; I am simply following her path and I will, until the day I leave this world.

All the while, I heard from several that I was crazy to do this. But my mind envisioned helping so many in the care centers, those people who *time* seemed to have forgotten. Over time, I asked several, from nursing homes to hospice how could anyone leave their "loved one" in a facility and simply walk away. I have yet to hear an answer from anyone. I did make peace with that question, though, many years later. I decided the person who would abandon their "loved one," only to return for their inheritance after their death, is the same person who abuses animals. They have no soul; they have no compassion; they have no idea that what they did will come around to haunt them. At the end of their days, they will be scrambling to make up for all the horrible things they did. They will fall short, as far as I am concerned. As everyone who leaves a path of wreckage behind them as they amble through life will soon learn, one is responsible for their actions.

I am one of the lucky ones. I will leave this world with no regrets, no, "Geez, I wish I would have…," or, "Why didn't I do that when I had the opportunity?". I will have done what was important to me. I don't have to explain being "obsessed" "overprotective" or "too focused" about the group that began with a little Great Dane who saved my life. Instead of "the nod," I just smile and ignore their complaints. After all, anyone who knows me will never sit in judgment of decisions I made in my personal life. They know I wrapped my life around making sure those in nursing homes, care centers, etc. are not forgotten. This is my dream - never anyone else's - so no explanation needed.

Jennie helped me find life again when I believed mine was over. There isn't a day that passes that I don't miss her. She is always with me, and she has led me to every one of my babies through the years. Absolute divine intervention.

From our beginning in Jennie's and my hometown of Omaha, Nebraska 30 years ago, Paws for Friendship members and I have seen such amazing opportunities to help by sharing our pets. We now de-stress many premed students ready to graduate, and they are told pet therapy can be prescribed instead of a pill, depending on an individual's need. We have professional members who bring their pets into sessions with patients! Often, the patient relaxes and is more open to therapy while petting a dog. Children in hospice are visited at home, and the unconditional love exchanged between a pet and a child is indescribable. The stories are plentiful because we have the best volunteers on earth--two-footed as well as four-footed!

We began visiting on a regular basis, and we were blessed with others who also wanted to share their precious babies. Nursing homes soon led to facilities that were once "off limits" to dogs. I experienced firsthand what it took legally to do this. I had a beautiful painting of a little duck gliding effortlessly across a pond. Very serene. You could get lost in the painting. What appeared to be relaxing, at first glance, revealed that the little duck was paddling his little feet off *under* the water, out of view. In a world of insurance, membership items, and technology to communicate with others across the world, I learned these were hidden from view. Had that little duck not wanted to cross that pond, he may have led a safe, easy life. But obviously he wanted to, he needed to cross, and so he did.

If I had to say what is the most important "thing" you could give someone, it would be your time. That is more valuable than gold or silver: the intangible luxury of your time. I have so many dear memories that they would fill an entire library.

I have visited with a parent and his daughter at a facility known to have problems with staffing. The dad was a professional in everyday life, the daughter going to school to become a therapist. Coming around a corner with my angel, Jennie, I stopped to witness something that has stayed with me for many years. A resident had fallen asleep at the table and his juice glass was still full, teetering on the table's edge. Without disrupting the resident, and without calling for an aide, this dad simply pushed the glass onto the table further so it would not fall. To save the resident any embarrassment from spilling the glass, this dad simply helped. Before the dad could leave to visit with others, the resident woke up and greeted this man, who had brought a family pet to visit. He smiled and started petting this little Boxer, and with the other hand reached for the glass of juice. After taking a few sips he smiled and said he was glad *he* placed it back far enough from the table's edge so it would not spill. He didn't want to cause *any* unnecessary work for the staff who were so good to him. The dad never mentioned what he did; neither did I.

Another precious memory from a visit began when a resident asked if "we" had eaten our dinner yet. She had just finished hers and was waiting for the babies to visit. Another member replied, it was fine and could always be reheated. She said her family understood, and not to give it another thought. The resident smiled and began hugging her baby. I remember seeing nothing but smiles and wagging tails. It was easy to see the connection that you could not purchase in any store or off any internet site. To attempt to explain why these are important would be like trying to explain a beautiful rainbow after a storm, or after a devastating tornado went through a community and nobody was hurt. Physical things were lost but were not what *really* mattered.

When our members find some quiet time, I hope they reflect as I do, remembering what mattered. How many lives they have changed with all their visits! I hope they remember all those faces who were so grateful they were there, and they just happened to have brought an angel with them.

For all the Hallmark cards ever made, all the commercials made to touch your heart, their lives have already been enriched tenfold. Our members' character includes the love they keep in their hearts from sharing their little angels. These traits define who *they* are and who *they* are is incredible; *they* define compassion. This is the sum total of what makes them who they are. I admire and respect them greatly for that.

AND TOTO TOO?

We met so many incredible people, gifts from God, to be honest. All loved Jennie and tolerated me, and that was fine with me. I could have cared less if anyone remembered my name, as long as they never forgot hers. Soon, years passed and as we welcomed many new people in our life. We met some that would always leave an imprint on our hearts. One person was recovering from a stroke, and we began our visits to the hospital he was in. Little did we know then, he was a Director of the Omaha Community Playhouse, and he loved Jennie. He told me, after he recovered and went back to work, he wanted to cast her in one of his plays. We were flattered of course; I, more than Jennie. She just seemed to absorb every opportunity that came along with grace and compassion.

A call from this lovely man, Charles Jones, came with an incredible opportunity. He wanted to cast her as "Toto" in The Wiz. Mind you, after meeting the cast, we realized she outweighed the actress who played Dorothy by over 40 pounds. The details were simple. I would wait with her in the wings of the stage, and when Dorothy would call for Toto, Jennie would run out and "hug" Dorothy by standing on her hind legs. It was quite a sight—she towered over Dorothy! The audience roared with laughter, and you could hear every gasp. After Dorothy gave her a treat, Jennie came back to me.

I soon found out regular treats were not going to do it anymore, so I began to cook for her. An assortment of meats would be cooked and given to Dorothy to give her with each performance. The entire cast embraced her, as did the staff and volunteers with the Playhouse. She would appear to "hold court" backstage after her performance, and she met her admirers with nothing but love. We had a wonderful time, and a medallion was made for her that said "Toto." She wore it on her gold collar with pride. She was listed in the play's program as Jennie of Idle Acres. (Idle Acres is what we called the acreage we lived on; Mom decided on that name. She said because none of the animals had to do anything other than be waited on and be loved, the acres were idle.) It worked for us, and looked very professional in the program, too. We stood proudly with the other cast members as the audience came to greet us. She even had a stamp with a BIG paw print on it so yes, they also had her autograph.

As our visits increased, so did opportunities for speaking engagements which we gladly accepted. These gave us an opportunity to talk about our program and recruit new members. Jennie was given many awards, and we were fearless on camera and in rooms filled with dignitaries there to hear about our program and the Great Dane that founded it. She took everything in stride and accepted all the praise with her ever-present grace and unconditional love. We opened chapters all over, each with loving pets shared with those in nursing homes, etc. by loving owners who also knew their babies could make a difference. One chapter in North Carolina had an article written about their volunteer service in the community. This was exciting to hear - front page color pictures and an article as well. We asked for a copy to frame, and the excitement grew closer to publishing time. After the paper was printed, I received a call from our coordinator who did the interview. She was crying and apologetic at first. I had no idea what happened because she was almost afraid to tell me.

After I reassured her everything was going to be fine, she said they printed my name wrong, and she thought I would be upset. I asked her if Jennie's name was spelled correctly. She said oh yes, she'd made sure she had given them the correct spelling. I began to laugh and told her I didn't care what they called me, as long as they spelled Jennie correctly. Soon, laughter broke out, and she realized I was serious and thanked me. I thanked her for everything she had done and was doing for Paws for Friendship, Incorporated. We did frame the article, and sure enough, Jennie's name is correct as the founder of our program, and I am mentioned as Pam. Pam's a good name.

Jennie and I had always preferred to visit nursing homes over other kinds of facilities. I think it was because the residents seemed to have toned us more. Hospital and outpatient facility patients usually had family and friends to visit them; not so much in nursing homes. The homes ran from affluent to those needing updating. We always gravitated to those needing an update.

Jennie seemed to know how fragile these residents were. She always walked up to them carefully, respectfully, and waited for any sign they wanted to pet her. She did know who would welcome her with open arms and who would give her several hugs. While they sat in wheelchairs, she appeared to be giant-sized when they pulled her close for a hug. If they could not reach her, she hugged their wheelchairs. She was as close as possible to let them know she was hugging them.

CHRISTMAS FROM THE HEART

While most people were enjoying Christmas Eve with family and friends, we made visits. My family was Jennie and many dear friends.

We met one lady right after she moved into a nursing home. We watched her move slowly through the room as we stopped to visit her. Her age was not normal: she was much younger than the other residents. She sat down and began to pet Jennie. She told me how beautiful she was and thanked us for visiting with her. As the years passed, we always made sure we visited with her. Her slow mobility had progressed to the point that she was almost bedridden. Her attempts to move around were obviously more and more painful.

Another year passed and, as usual, we made our Christmas Eve visits. Several of my friends had stopped asking why I was spending Christmas Eve in a nursing home. I had told them I felt I needed to be there; that Jennie had opened a new world for me because she knew, long before I did, that we needed to be there. We walked into our special friend's room knowing that time and Muscular Dystrophy had stolen her ability to get out of bed without help; had stolen her independence. She used her uncompromised muscles as best she could.

Little did we know, when she greeted us with a big smile, that she had a surprise for us. I have had many treasures in my life that were more valuable, but I was about to witness one that would stay with me forever. She had gotten a staff member to get her some yarn months earlier. She said, "Because you both never forgot about visiting me, I wanted to give you something." After repeating several times, "It's not much," and "I hope you like it," she handed me a knitted collar for Jennie. With hands that were at times uncontrollable, and with more pain than I could imagine, she had made Jennie a collar. She said, "I love this little angel, and I wanted to give her something." I put it on her and it fit perfectly. Jennie put her head on the bed so our friend could pet her. She nuzzled in as if to thank her for this incredible gift. Finding words was almost impossible for me. We both cried and smiled at each other.

We treasured that gift that was measured by the heart. Jennie only wore the collar when we went to see our friend. It made her so happy to know it was perfectly made to fit an angel. Our friend passed away that following spring, and we went to her funeral. Jennie wore the collar for the last time. It is a priceless treasure, a dear memory of a friend we met on our Christmas Eve visits to those who time seems to have forgotten.

WHY ARE YOU HERE?

Reviewing your life gives you time to think about basic, important questions. Who are you? What is your place in the world? What is your meaning and purpose? Where has your path taken you? It gives you a chance to think about whether the assumptions you have made about your life have been wrong, or whether it is possible to forgive people who have hurt or betrayed you. You may even end up reframing some of the major events in your life so that your story is rebalanced with the positive as well as the negative. Not to worry, you still have time.

DOWNSIDE TO PET THERAPY

There has always been one downside to pet therapy. There are not enough hours in a day to reach everyone in need. We were visiting critical care facilities, VA facilities, hospitals, and nursing homes. I can honestly say my heart will always be in the nursing homes. Too often families walk away and continue their life without visiting their "loved ones" they placed in those facilities. But many are certainly there when their inheritance comes around. I have asked many professionals in the medical field how someone can do that to their loved one. I have yet to get a reply that explains it, and 30 years later I am still looking for that answer. I have come to believe an idea about animal abusers. They are the kind that would leave their loved ones in care centers and walk away. Many hospice facilities have told me at times they have to sue the families for them to claim their loved ones after they have passed away.

Mind you, I am far from a Rhodes Scholar, but I do know the difference between right and wrong. That is so wrong on so many levels. From a well-lived childhood in what I would consider the land of OZ, through visiting many facilities, I have seen a world I never knew existed. Maybe Jennie knew the adventures we shared would teach me a lesson I would never have learned. Some people are just plain mean. I do know they will leave this world with regrets and will be unable to make up for the scorched path they left behind. It baffles my mind as the reality is crystal clear. Jennie gave me that.

She taught me more things than can ever be counted, introduced many friends I would never have met, and taught me how to live with a broken heart.

So many take things for granted. I've learned everything can be gone in an instant and to be grateful for every blessing. I have had so many in my lifetime they are uncountable, immeasurable.

CAN MY DOG DO THIS?

You may have decided you want to share your precious little angel for many reasons, from personal to professional. Many of our members were doubtful they would be able to visit because they thought their baby was too "excitable," or "not mature enough." Many were told certain requirements must be met before their pet could even be considered a therapy pet. All the classes in the world cannot make a therapy pet. *YOU* made them therapy pets by loving and caring for them beyond the definition of the words. *You* made them 'love sponges' because *you* made them part of your family. Then *you* went one step further: *you* decided to share their love with others. Socialization is our focus, as well as a loving disposition and a desire to meet new people and pets. Basic obedience is always welcome. It's a great opportunity to learn new things and be around other pets also eager to learn. If you haven't socialized your pet, please do so. It is through trust in you that they feel safe in new environments. A wheelchair is not a monster; a walker coming towards them should not be feared. If you have taught them basic skills and they trust you, you are halfway there.

I have seen so many surprised looks through the years, once our members have seen for themselves the unconditional love their babies were giving to complete strangers. Hands curled through the years from rheumatoid arthritis were opened as best as they could be, to pet their little angel. No question about it, they are the closest on earth to a real angel. Being their "designated driver" is an honor. Had you not made the decision to share them, knowing what you know now, what a loss to all. From the residents, patients, and staff you visit, remember all the sighs, smiles, and hand clasping when your little angel comes into view. The anticipation only grows when tails are wagging, and wiggles are seen at an all-time high. *YOU* made the difference; *YOU* chose to open your heart to share this little miracle you adore at home.

Bless their hearts, rescues of all types can bring 'baggage' with them when you adopt them. Some of that baggage is positive, and some can be beyond words to describe how anyone could do this to an animal. Anything could trigger it, and that is why many try to hide behind you. Many are already anticipating that something bad is going to happen. With LOTS of patience, they will learn that they finally are safe and do not have to worry anymore. Just be always aware of their surroundings until they feel comfortable with you and their new home. They will need reassurance from you that they will be ok, and then they can be introduced to things, people and pets that will not hurt them. Patience is the key here, and don't let ANYONE rush you; this is all on their schedule now. When you adopted them, you made a lifetime commitment, so please do NOT bring them into your life unless you can give them a wonderful life. They will only be with you for a short time over your lifetime. Love them beyond the definition of the word. Never forget our beloved Founder was a rescue. Look what she accomplished when she finally knew nobody would ever hurt her again. She even saved my life when I thought all was lost.

GATHERING ROSES IN WINTER

When a stranger in a care center glances your way on your first visit, you hope they want to see your baby and pet them. Often you are met with no response, and you move on. The next time you visit, this stranger just may speak to your pet or you. You think *progress* and each time you visit, things get more comfortable. With your determination to make these visits, strangers become part of your life, as friends. They matter to you and most of all they matter to your pet. Schedules are rearranged to make these visits; dinners served earlier or later now have become the norm. Changing your schedules around in your life to make sure you visit before visiting hours are over becomes second nature to you. You remember the resident who asked you to wake them up if they are sleeping, just to see your pet. Remembering something so simple as helping someone place their empty juice glass on the table quietly, to call no attention to it. The resident may not have the reach they once had; arthritis has stolen it through the years.

The last thing you would ever want to do is to embarrass them, as they are aware of the toll illness or age has taken on their life. The residents feel the grace and respect you show them. If their voice has been erased because of illness or time, their smile, their nod acknowledges your kindness. Believe me they never forget you were kind to them. An expression can speak volumes. Alzheimer's comes into a person's life like a thief. It steals precious moments away that were safely kept in the heart. We have always visited a variety of facilities because their needs were different. In many facilities, needs meant just sitting quietly while someone pets your dog. No words were spoken – just the language of caring and compassion through your pet. Other times, just listening to stories told to you by someone who has lived a full life and just needs someone to listen.

It always amazes me when we are contacted by a student who needs Community Service Hours. You can tell most of their parents had to drag them to the facility. Most had never been in a facility where elderly live. Most had no idea how loneliness can consume someone's life as it is coming to an end.

After the visit I would get a call from the student asking me if I knew that one guy drove a tank in the war. Did I know that lady in the corner room used to be a nurse in the war? Did I know that guy who sat by the window in the main room used to be a tank mechanic? Did I know? Did I know? I loved those questions, and my answer was always the same. They are living history; you cannot find those stories in any book compared to talking to someone who was there. Our Community Service Hour students multiplied quickly much to everyone's delight.

We have received many letters and cards through the years from families that thank us for making a difference in their loved one's life. These are the real valuables in life, those worth more than anything you could ever deposit in any bank. You will understand why if you have ever had a bad day, a day where nothing seems to make sense. You need to just stop and remember all the smiles you have given away. Strangers that are now friends should come into focus to ease your day. Their limbs may be missing, their speech impaired, their eyesight failing but the pride they have in your friendship should always fill your heart. Our members have made it possible to reach around the world with their unending compassion and generosity.

"It takes a village" sounds so simple, but it encompasses so much more. Sharing in each other's heartbreak when we lose a precious little angel brings the reality of the fact they just can't stay long enough; they never could. We are all bound together by the precious gift of friendship. Choices come and go in our lives, and the opportunities are endless as to how we spend our time. Please remember that the lives you have touched will be grateful forever and a day to you. You took time to talk to them; you took time to raise their lap robe up to cover their amputated limbs. You never said a word, but your smile spoke the best language possible. Theirs back to you said it all.

A very wise person told me long ago, "Memory is the power to gather roses in winter," and that stands tried and true today.

Now that the die has been cast, you have all those memories in your heart that will stay with you forever. I remember many times our group has saved my life. You have become a family to me and there will never be enough ways to thank you for that. We are the perfect picture of "It takes a village." It always has and always will.

THE LEGALITIES

Nobody is special; nobody is above another in our organization. Yes, titles are titles because in a real-world, society structures this, and we must comply. I never kidded myself: it takes sacrifice of several things to be the only Registered Agent of our group. Basically, when I made a promise 30 years ago, I knew I would honor that promise as long as I drew a breath. I have been told *our* group is a rarity. For 30 years we have held true to our mission; we have honored our organization where few ever did – much less for 30 years. I cannot begin to tell you how proud and grateful I am of all our members; they have made this possible. We register each year in Nebraska because we were founded there. I make a special trip to the State Capital Building just to renew in person and *still* find myself humbled by all we have accomplished. We file in Florida because that is where headquarters is now. That may change as time goes on. I hope they realize the pace they have set many others only try to achieve. Thirty years has become a reality because of *our members* sharing their little angels.

I hear from some of our officers, and we have had several officers through the years. I don't want my address listed, nor my personal phone number and I am certainly not going to be 'available' 24 hours a day, 7 days a week like YOU are. That is why we don't keep officers long, because I let them know IF there's a problem or the possibility of a problem, you MUST be available 24/7. Time zones could bring a question needing an answer right away, not between 9 and 5 Monday through Friday. Everyone thinking they are ready to take the helm should rethink their idea quickly. I remind them that, if the group cannot afford something needed, they will be paying for it, and hope to get reimbursed when the group can pay for it. As you can imagine, THAT went over like a lead balloon.

It still amazes me how some think a title gives them power. I've never figured that one out. I remind everyone that no one is more important than the other; it truly "takes a village." Some act like I'm crazy but they know I am not kidding. There are no awards given, no records broken, no medals worn at the end of the day. The reward is knowing you have something more precious than gold and silver, something that has no value in dollars and cents. It is much more valuable than that: you know in your heart that you made a difference. No ticker tape parades, just knowing what you did just may have helped someone get through an awful day. Someone may have felt hopeless until you arrived with an angel on four legs, and they knew you were Heaven sent. One can never lose hope. I have heard many say they can handle what I do, no problem. But then as they learn their little feet will be paddling as fast as they can, behind the scenes, to cross every "pond" we encounter, and it must look as effortless as that little Mallard duck does.

Believe me, I have spent many hours trying to make sure nothing changes. Someone else will have all the file cabinets; they will have totes full of records dating from October 1993 when we began. They will store all the items we have, and they will have to carry on the legacy Jennie started. When the doctor told me to get my affairs in order, when I was diagnosed with stage three cancer, you cannot imagine the whirlpool going through my mind. I survived that and onward we go. I have a manual I have written through the years with step-by-step instructions, and I am praying that it will be respected for what it is: a legacy that will never end. Generations will welcome our babies into their lives, and I believe with all my heart I will find the right hands in which to place the manual before I leave this world. I have faith. You must always have faith.

I have wrapped 30 years of my life around our group and only when I leave this world will I "retire." I am a firm believer that there are other worlds to sing in, so I will continue my passion wherever God sends me.

Our group gives me oxygen, and it has saved my life many times through Jennie. She is always beside me, always in my heart. I know this was never anyone else's dream and I know nobody will have the commitment I do. It's funny looking back, so many have said, "When are you stepping down? We can handle it, so go ahead................" They mean well, BUT when reality lands, it's a completely different matter.

I looked beyond the legal "official" work and saw faces that would be affected. I remember making promises to come visit again, I remember those who thanked me for taking time *just to talk to them.* They made *me* feel special because they loved my baby and offered what little they had as a treat to my baby for being there. Bingo games offered many prizes, from personal items to simple treasures to hold on to. Too often crackers, cookies, chips were chosen because they wanted to give *our* babies "something" to show how grateful they were that we visited them. Total all those experiences up and make a chart or a graph of that. Compare them side by side with cold facts and explain to me why we should ignore those faces for the cold hard reality of running a nonprofit.

IT'S PERSONAL

I have spent a lot of time reflecting through the years and realized I have *so* much to be grateful for. My gratitude is simple, I've taken time to count the blessings I have. When so many have lost their precious little angels, they hold them dear in their hearts as I have for all my babies that have gone before me. Our hearts all break for those who have lost their little angels. I heard a comment that I should not announce when we lose a pet. Nobody wanted to know. We honor *them* in memorials because they *have* earned our respect. Our group would not be the group it is without them. Each angel represents the absolute best of us. They are our foundation every bit as Jennie is and they deserve our respect. It is *my* honor to write their memorials and it is also the hardest thing I do.

REFLECTIONS OF FAITH

Faith is believing in things when common sense tells you not to. This quote is from a movie I watch every year, Miracle on 34th Street. It's a classic and I enjoy the classics, especially at Christmas time. Through the years my faith in God has flourished; my faith in people, some people, has been tested but remains steadfast. Christmas is my favorite season, full of hope and promise. I realized an awfully long time ago it is not the presents; it isn't the parties; it is the luxury of time given to someone you deeply care about. My family is all gone now, but I have incredible friends who make this season special. I will always go home for Christmas in my heart. If I could send everyone a wish it would be that you would take a moment and realize how many lives you have touched by sharing your little angels. Being their designated driver is critical to your mission of helping those in need, one paw at a time. In case you don't realize the impact you have made, let me remind you. Your dedication to brighten someone's day has inspired several to join, opening many new chapters throughout the nation. Because of you, many who have not had a reason to smile in an awfully long time now share stories of your baby visiting. We realize there are other organizations out there that they could have joined. We are very grateful they joined Paws for Friendship Inc. We are separate from all of them for a good reason.

Our focus is on the residents and patients. It always has been and always will be. We understand how important the visits are to those in the facilities we visit. Our members have made 30 years possible. They may not realize it, but more lives are touched than they will ever know. Our members have inspired me in ways I cannot begin to explain or thank them for. My life is rich in blessings, memories of faces now gone, and stories forever etched in my heart. Our members have not only changed my life but theirs as well. They will not forget the stories told to them, the smiles exchanged between a stranger and now a friend. Their babies have touched so many lives just by offering their unconditional love.

Please know the gift our members have given to those in the facilities cannot be deposited in any bank nor can it be given a dollar amount. It is priceless, and they are responsible for that. Every time they make a visit, they are increasing the value of what they hold dear. Words are inadequate to describe what they have done by sharing their little angels.

Many will go through life searching for a purpose and many will never give it a thought. Many will not even think of leaving a legacy as everyone should in some way or another. The riches someone values differ greatly depending on who you are thinking of. The riches I value are from what our members have given me throughout these 30 years. Every Brinks truck on the planet could not carry them, no bank could ever contain them, and no calculator could ever reach that amount. Priceless is a word to describe what riches they have given me. Being grateful is just not enough to say to you. Please know every life touched by sharing their little angel has also touched mine.

MORE REFLECTIONS...

As years passed, we grew by God's grace into communities all over, sharing our loving pets. I like to think people take time to read Jennie's Story on our website. That tells our story and the fact that we would not be here without her. I never had the strength she did, I never had the heart she did, and it's a fact I would not be here today if it weren't for her. Some might think she was just a dog, just a rescue who needed someone to love her. Some may say that. I can tell you without hesitation, anyone who knew us, who saw us in visiting facilities, knew the truth. I was simply her "designated driver;" we were on her path of travel from day one. Thirty years later I am still on her path of travel.

We welcomed many rescues into our home, and all gave her the respect she deserved and earned. She set the pace, and everyone followed behind her. If she wanted to be on the couch, they would move for her, and then after she got comfortable, they would slowly crawl up to be next to her. I watched in amazement the respect they knew she deserved, all without question. There is a reason GOD spelled backwards is DOG.

She just took your breath away when she visited. It was watching pure love given to total strangers. In the early years we visited children's facilities where many were in leg braces made of metal and leather. I remember a little girl so excited to meet her, she almost fell trying to get close to Jennie. Awkward with the crutches, she struggled to gain control, all the while she was using Jennie to help. Jennie stood as a statue, never moving a muscle all the while this little girl, unknowingly, pushed against her and brushed her with the crutches. She never moved and just looked at me as if to let me know the little girl was not hurting her. She just knew she was helping by standing perfectly still. I had never witnessed something like that before. It was as if she knew if she had moved the little girl would have fallen. Jennie had more love and compassion than any animal or person I had ever known. I was watching an angel at work.

We were invited to so many events in the community. Jennie was honored at several of them. I could tell all about how this angel saved my life, and how she brought hope and joy back to several who time and families seemed to have forgotten. I would take her lead off, and she would walk the room "greeting" everyone. Every so often she would glance my way, making sure I knew she was there for me. I was invincible when she was there, and she knew it. I do not speak at events anymore, I simply can't. Inevitably, the facts of how we began would need to be answered, and without her I just can't find the words. They are always in my heart; I just cannot talk about them without falling apart.

We have received many Christmas cards and letters from parents and families telling of how grateful they were to us for brightening up their loved ones' lives with our visits. I always reply that Jennie shared her love with everyone she had ever met, and we were grateful we could be there for their loved ones. The overwhelming majority of the cards for 11 ½ years were always addressed to Jennie. Maybe I was mentioned, often not. That was simply fine with me. Every card was displayed proudly.

RETIREMENT

I could never explain it, I just always knew it was there. She *was* an angel, and she touched each person she met in a way hard to describe. Words were hard to find. My eyes saw an angel at work; my ears heard the loving words spoken to her. I thought about conversations we had, road trips we did, while working to heal lonely hearts, so many full of despair. While I watched time take a toll on Jennie, and watched her steps taken more carefully, I knew it was time to retire her and let her relax and enjoy all she had accomplished. She was not in agreement with my decision. I had introduced my other babies into the world of pet therapy, and Jennie had always supervised their training. Each time we went out the front door Jennie stared at me as if to say, "What about me?".

More tears were shed as I tried to explain why she had to retire; why she earned her retirement. We were never in agreement, but I started not visiting because I saw the disappointment in her eyes. She seemed content with that. As the years passed, we stopped making visits. Our focus was more on staying home and pushing paperwork around. It seemed easier to let the others visit while we started to take it easy. Retirement was not a word well received by her; with each day came a new challenge to go for a drive but not make a visit. I tried between the tears to get her to understand she needed to slow down. That was never in her vocabulary, and that fact never changed.

We were blessed with so many incredible members that I knew each facility was well visited. So, Jennie and I focused on our paperwork, growing the group she founded, reaching into new areas once off limits to a dog. When I think of how far we have come in thirty years, I remember each step along the way as if it were yesterday. How silly it seemed that so many places were once off limits, now that they opened their doors wide for us.

NO GOODBYES

As you can imagine, when my eyes could no longer ignore what I was seeing, and the medicines were of no comfort anymore, Jennie continued to comfort me as I held her and cried, knowing the time would arrive when I had to make the decision: not a goodbye decision, only an "I need to send you to Heaven to rest," decision. I explained to her that I knew she would be waiting for me when I got there. It's a decision I can still feel today, in a heart that is still broken, even though many paw prints have come and gone in my life. What do you do when you know the saddest moment in your life is when the one who gave you the best memories becomes a memory?

After 11 ½ years living with an angel, never forgetting she saved my life when all seemed hopeless, I knew I owed her the dignity she had more than earned. God needed her, so I held her as she crossed into Heaven to send her home. I think of her now, visiting with all those who have gone before me, laying in pastures full of the most beautiful flowers never found in this world. They are only found in Heaven. Colors never seen here, only there. Gentle breezes surrounded by a true, pure love only God can make you feel. I know she will greet me someday, and we will never be separated again. What a glorious day that will be! She is with me every day; I can feel her around me. She is the heart of an organization she founded thirty years ago.

Many will tell you I am obsessed with this organization; I will admit I am. I am protecting Jennie's legacy and will with all that I am. I have wrapped thirty years of my life around it and will continue until I draw my last breath. Many babies have come into my life, and I have adored them all. They all played a part in shaping my life. None will ever come close to Jennie and that is a fact. Jennie knew I needed her to help me find a reason to live. She gave me that, and in honor of her I have devoted my life to the organization she founded. There isn't a day that passes that I don't miss her. I believe if you hold your loved ones within your heart, you *are* there with them. No distance can ever keep you away, no matter what. My life and the lives of thousands of others were affected in a profoundly positive way by a little rescued Great Dane puppy who knew she had a purpose and lived to see it come to fruition.

I am in the autumn of my life and choose not to fear it. I choose to embrace it and be grateful I am still here to make that choice. I know there are other worlds to sing in, so there is no fear. I know I will see Jennie, and she will look at me with those beautiful eyes, and together we will be grateful for each of those incredible 11-1/2 years in which she changed so many lives, including mine. So many have touched my life in one way or another, and I am grateful beyond words. I still believe people join our group to make a difference in the world. I believe everyone must leave a legacy. You are in charge of what your legacy will be. You all know mine, so that is without question. What will yours be?

On November 8, 1999, our beloved founder, Jennie, passed away. Her heart and soul continue to guide this organization. Her legacy will live through generations helping those in need.

HER NAME WAS JENNIE

When you were once lost
And unsure of your way
A Dane came along
And convinced you to stay

And her name was Jennie

You taught her to trust
She brought you her love
You were gifts to each other
Given by someone above

And through all your love
An idea was born
You'd visit the people
Who were sad and forlorn

She extended her paw
And you gave your hand
And organized others
All over the land

Jan Schmidt

The group provides warmth
Through its tail wagging pets
Unconditional love
Is as good as it gets

Her legend lives on
In this group she began
Through the hard work of others
And her beloved friend Jan

And her name was Jennie.

– by a dear friend, Trudi Shiverdecker,
                                       in memory of Jennie, 11-8-99

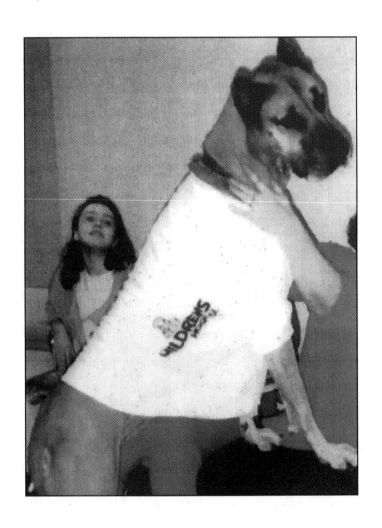

PART II

TESTIMONIES OF LOVE

DUDE

I moved to Omaha seven years ago and was hoping to get my Yellow Lab, Dude, involved in pet therapy. My sister who lives in Omaha, knew a lady who volunteered with her dog for Paws for Friendship. I contacted her and we met up at a facility in Papillion where she could evaluate Dude. Of course, he passed with flying colors and we were excited to see where our fit would be. I started out visiting the retirement home where my mother lived. Even though it was fun to see her, the ladies were finicky and most didn't really appreciate the pet therapy visits.

I soon moved on to visiting a memory care facility, a hospice facility and for some reason, the "fit" wasn't quite right. I hate to say it – Dude can brighten anyone's day, but when the facility doesn't even know you are there, it just didn't sit right with me. Dude did occasional visits to an elementary school, University of Nebraska Medical Center (UNMC), and we even visited an insurance agency to give their employees a mental break on a Friday afternoon.

I always wanted to volunteer at Methodist Hospital, and the schedule we had at the time showed visits on the weekend only. Then in October of 2017, they started a new pet therapy pilot program where dogs would visit floors that weren't serviced on the weekends. Dude and I signed up and the rest is history! Thanks to Dude and his pal, Lexi, the pilot program was approved! We now visit Methodist Hospital every Wednesday at 1:00 pm and we visit patients on the 6th floor, which is oncology and step-down ICU.

We are so happy to be back at Methodist Hospital on a regular basis now after Covid interrupted our visits for some time. We also continue to visit Methodist College and UNMC when requested. The reason I'm so happy with Methodist Hospital is because they have a fantastic volunteer program and coordinator. We feel so appreciated in visiting there, it makes it a win–win situation for all! Almost everyone in the hospital knows who Dude is now and I'll often hear staff members say, "There's Dude – he's a legend around here!"

Another note – Dude was featured on the WOW6 News in Sept. 2022. He had a cancerous growth removed from his mouth this past summer, so they did a story about him visiting cancer patients and how they can relate to each other after his own bout with cancer. Below is a link to the story. It is very touching and the TV station did such a great job!

https://www.wowt.com/2022/09/15/dude-therapy-dog-forms-special-bond-with-cancer-patients/

Linda Norling, Nebraska, Paws Member

STANLEY

When my husband and I lost our last big hunting dog, we were not planning on getting another dog. But as I contemplated what was next after retiring from traveling as a children's entertainer/ventriloquist, I was drawn to the work that another fellow ventriloquist was doing with pet therapy through Paws for Friendship. After hearing about it, I knew this was my "what's next." After a visit to a local breeder, I knew Stanley was the right dog, but never dreamed how perfect he would be.

Stanley started "work" right away as he accompanied me while visiting my mother-in-law during her final days on earth. Stanley brought joy to the other nursing home residents too. He also joined my performances as part of my "cast", interacting with puppets and acting out stories. As we continued in our journey with Paws, we started visiting libraries and schools so children could read to Stanley. It has been a huge blessing and has made my retirement from entertaining much easier because we are still bringing smiles to children.

One time, a sight-impaired child wrote a story about Stanley in Braille and brought it to the library to read to him. She gave me the story to keep, and it is such a treasure!! A number of children have also written their own stories/books about Stanley to read to him during our visits. I, too, have started writing children's books about Stanley for the children to read on our visits to libraries and schools.

The joy that Stanley brings to those we visit is very obvious and is a gift to me as well. Parents and teachers often tell me how much Stanley's visits mean to the children. They send photos and quotes which prove the value of pet therapy. Volunteer work with Paws for Friendship has been a gift to me, to Stanley, and to all the children and families who have spent time with Stanley. I am grateful for this very fulfilling next chapter in my life.

Lisa Laird, Iowa, Paws member

HERKY

I want to share a little with you about our Border Collie Australian Shepherd mix, Herky. He has been loving life as a therapy dog for six and a half years.

I also belong to a teacher organization, and our guest speaker one evening was a member of Paws for Friendship with her Corgi, Cooper. Throughout her talk, I knew that Herky was born to do this sort of "work". Within a couple of months, Herky was approved and was so excited to begin his mission.

We used to go to Eastern Nebraska Veterans' Home, but we have not returned since the Covid shutdown. That's okay because we keep busy visiting Hillcrest Health and Rehab (HHR) every Friday night. Also, about once a week, Herky and I go to the Lewis and Clark Middle School in Bellevue. Every once in a while, we answer the call to go somewhere else when asked. I get home from work so Herky can go to "work". No one enjoys the visits more than him!! The residents at HR look forward to Fridays as well. Everyone knows Herky's name, but not everyone knows mine!! That's fine with me, because I am not the star of the show!

Over the years we have experienced some amazing moments: tears of happiness, a lot of stories about former pets, pets they miss or had to give up when entering rehab, and luckily, so much laughter! Herky has personality plus, and he knows just who needs extra attention and love. I am so proud of him during every single visit, as he gives his all and truly enjoys every minute.

And Herky loves going to school. He trots down the hall, and once he hears the collective "awwww" from an open classroom door, he invites himself in and makes his way up and down every aisle. Class stops, but no one seems to care. Several teachers even keep treats for Herky in their desks.

I am so proud to be a member of Paws for Friendship. Sharing Herky with so many people has truly been a blessing.

Teri Clapper, Nebraska, Paws Member

ESMERALDA AND ZAHARA

Back in 2004, we got our first Newfoundland puppy, Isadora. She was such a people pup that we thought she would be good at therapy work and it would give her purpose. We joined another organization and did all the training required. We drove hours each way to be evaluated. During that time, we met Jan and Paws at the St. Petersburg Saturday Market. Isadora loved Jan and so we switched over to Paws for Friendship and never looked back.

Newfoundlands are such a sweet and gentle breed. Isadora visited nursing homes and was part of the Paws to Read program when it started. During the past years, Isadora trained Ursula; Ursula trained Esmeralda; and Esmeralda is now training Zahara. Although we lost Isadora in 2014 and Ursula in 2021, we still treasure memories of them.

Ursula and Esmeralda used to work together at the Albany International Airport in Albany, New York as canine ambassadors until Ursula's hips made it too hard for her to get around. Esmeralda was still working at the airport until Covid hit.

Esmeralda loves kids, so we have done elementary and pre-school programs and Paws to Read. She has also been a part of the Gasparilla Children's Parade when we had the train, and she has done nursing homes and rehabilitation centers where she dressed up like Santa and did photos with the residents. She also does PI day at the math lab at St. Petersburg College and she does therapy work for the LBGTQ+ Metro organization in St. Petersburg with Zahara.

My favorite visit of all time was at a nursing home in Pinellas Park with Isadora. We were there to visit, and Isadora walked up to a man in a wheelchair in the hallway who was blind and deaf. When she stopped in front of him and brushed his leg, he reached out to "see" what it was. When he felt her fur, his whole face lit up and he smiled. He rubbed her for a very long time, just stroking her back as she stood perfectly still. When he was done, he bent down and hugged her and smiled, nodded and patted her to move along. We never saw him there again, but those five minutes will stay with me forever. It has probably been fifteen years since that day, and the memory still brings tears to my eyes. I am very happy to be able to share my girls with those who need a hug.

Kate Brass, Florida, Paws Member

GOUDA ANNE AND SYROS PALMER

When I joined Paws for Friendship over ten years ago, I was searching for a therapy dog group that would fit my dogs and me. You see, I am blind, and I travel about my life with their help every day. I had looked at several groups, and because of my blindness, I was always told I had to have another dog – in addition to my seeing eye dogs. Wrong answer. I did my research, and I found Paws for Friendship.

I was blessed to find this group. They welcomed me with open arms. I have received numerous outstanding awards for the work that my dogs and I have accomplished. We go into non-profits and help to develop our community to make it better for all people and populations. I teach students that are blind and hearing impaired. I train them with orientation and mobility skills that help them to navigate their environment. Then I teach them how to work with the service dogs they have. They are spoken to in English and German, and they also sign to the dogs.

We do the usual duties of a therapy dog program. We visit, de-stress students, visit nursing homes, hospitals, and reading programs in the various non-profits and public libraries. Being an American Disability Advocate, I try to let society understand we must be included into society, and we have a lot to offer. I am proud that I was instrumental in changing a policy of the American Kennel Club that stated that service dogs could not be dual certified as therapy dogs. My first two black beauties, Mazie Grace and Tessa Mae, were two of the first recognized in this dual capacity.

I currently have two service dogs for the blind and hearing impaired, Gouda Anne and Syros Palmer. Gouda Anne, a Belgian Malinois, was a certified K-9 attack dog whose handler died. She was scavenging off the land when she was rescued. I took her in and retrained her. She now understands French, German, English, and sign language. Her three-year-old brother, a yellow Labrador, Syros Palmer, is my guide dog. Both dogs will soon complete their certification as therapy dogs, to compliment their service dog designation.

Paws for Friendship has helped me to have a better platform for my dogs and for people with disabilities. I appreciate Jan and Paws because they took a chance with me, and we have opened a lot of doors for all. I travel all over my state where my dogs are known in the transit systems, hospitals, schools, libraries, and our university campus. We share our love and message with wagging tails of kindness and wet juicy kisses. We love our job!

Beverly and Donnie Hammett, Mississippi, Paws Members

JOURNI AND LEGEND

I've been interested in doing pet therapy since around 1997. I started with a different organization with my one-year-old Golden Retriever, Jessie, and we often visited Woodbury Nursing Home and Rehabilitation Center in Woodbury, New York. One of my first memorable experiences was meeting two patients who were husband and wife. I can hear the husband's voice to this day talking about his Golden Retriever named Champ. His wife said that Champ was her husband's world. I knew that just by how he spoke of Champ and told stories about him. I loved to listen to his stories because Champ made him so happy. One day, sadly, just the wife was there, but she still enjoyed seeing Jessie.

Jessie and I also visited BelAire Nursing Home in Bellmore, New York. We met a gentleman there who used to be a fireman. His name was Bill. We always visited Bill and would spend a good amount of time chichatting as Jessie let Bill pet her. After our visit with Bill, we would always stop to say hello to a lady who sat in her doorway and she would tell Jessie that she liked her nose.

Then there was a visit that I will never forget. We visited a lady who was ill and not doing very well. She talked to Jessie and petted her. After some time, the lady became tired and we told her we would be back the next week to visit again. When we came back the next week, a lady stopped me in the hallway and asked if I had visited her mom the week before and she gave me the room number. I told her, "Yes, that was us." She thanked me and told me that her mom had passed away. She said her mom had told her that a dog came to visit her and that was her "angel in fur". What a moment! I was speechless and my breath was taken away. I could not believe what she was telling me! After that, I brought one of Jessie's sweatshirts to a store to have "Angel in Fur" embroidered on the back. It brings me comfort to know Jessie and I were there for this lady without even knowing how much the visit truly meant to her.

About three years after Jessie passed away at 10 years old, my next Golden Retriever, Destiny, did some pet therapy with the same organization and continued at the Woodbury Nursing Home for a few years. But it wasn't until I started my younger Golden Retriever, Journi, doing pet therapy at two years old when I learned about Paws for Friendship. I was looking for a different organization that was more personal and friendly to the volunteers. Our Noseworks instructor told me about Paws, and I reached out to one of the evaluators. Before I knew it, Journi and I were members of this wonderful organization and have been since 2016.

Journi is an exceptional pet therapy dog in my eyes. I knew she was liked at Woodbury, but I didn't realize just how much until one of our visits when Journi and I walked in the front door, and I heard a few voices yell out, "There's Journi!" "Journi, come over here!" "Journi, come and see me!" I was blown away! Journi once visited a lady who began crying with happiness after seeing her. The patient was happy to see Journi, but missed the companionship of her own dog so badly. She said the visit from Journi was just what she needed that day.

There once was also a very quiet man, sitting alone in the recreation room. I walked over and told him Journi and I came to visit him today. I asked him if he'd like to pet her and he smiled and started petting her. He didn't talk much. Journi and I stayed with him for about 20 minutes until I guess his hand got tired.

I have recently started taking my two-year-old Golden Retriever, Legend, to Woodbury as well. He does very well and he likes people. He hasn't had enough visits yet to have stories to tell, but I know they will be coming!

To sum it up, I can't explain how enlightening it is to see a patient who shows no interest or emotion as they see us walking down the hall towards them and they suddenly light up. I tell them we came by to see THEM; to say hello to THEM; to invite THEM to touch and pet the soft, gentle dog. Seeing their satisfaction and watching the patient light up, makes ME smile all the way home.

I love Paws for Friendship, and Jan Schmidt is truly amazing. I love her emails to all members with weekly updates and reminders. She is so accessible, and you can email her whenever you have a question or if you just want to tell her about a wonderful pet therapy experience.

Darlene Dambra, New York, Paws Member

MICKEY

Mickey is a pure-bred Mi-Ki. The Mi-Ki has its origins in the late 1980's and are bred to be intelligent, affectionate, calm, and loving. A cross between the Japanese Chin, Maltese, and Papillon, ensures therapy dog disposition.

When we first got Mickey, we did not specifically think of him as a therapy pet. We have a special needs grandson and soon realized the impact Mickey had on our grandson. As a result, Mickey started out as a therapy dog to our family.

After working with a trainer, he suggested Mickey could be a therapy dog and introduced us to Paws For Friendship. Mickey started his career in a nursing home. So many of the residents just wanted to hold and cuddle him. One of Mickey's advantages is his small size at five pounds. Residents can hold him comfortably. This turns out to be a problem because they do not want to give him up. It's almost like we need a timer to move him to the next person!

Mickey then participated in the Military Fresh Check Day which is a program to promote good mental health among U.S. Coast Guard cadets. It was so amusing to see cadets surrounding Mickey, playing with him and holding him. Many said how much they missed their own pets and how wonderful it was to see him.

Another adventure was participating in the annual charity Firefighters Stair Climb. Mickey was a huge hit and could easily fit in their helmets.

Mickey is also an official therapy dog at our local hospital. He even has his own ID badge. He is so at home there, and just walks around the nurse's stations greeting everyone. His picture is on bulletin boards and the computers of many employees. He is also part of a program for resident doctors to help them ease the tension during exam times.

Mickey also visits the patients at the hospital and cancer center. The patients will first see me enter the room, then their eyes light up when I lift Mickey onto the bed. One patient was in so much pain and commented how holding him eased the pain.

Finally, Mickey has introduced us to the world of therapy work giving love and joy to everyone.

Kathleen & Ronald Lesniak, Connecticut, Paws Members

ANDY

Our journey began in 2009 when I had a Labradoodle named Rufus who was born in 2004. After completing an advanced obedience course involving good citizenship training, I learned about him becoming a therapy dog. I contacted a very well-known therapy organization in October 2009, submitted the appropriate paperwork and dues, but I never heard back from them. Long story, short - I was ultimately told that Rufus and I were not good candidates for their organization.

I refused to be discouraged, and I decided I needed to find a therapy dog organization for Rufus to participate in. After researching various organizations I found Paws for Friendship. I called and talked in length with Jan Schmidt who was more than happy to have us join to be representatives in Ohio. Upon receiving the appropriate paperwork, we started searching for a facility for Rufus to visit.

Our first facility was First Community Village in Columbus, Ohio. Rufus started visiting this facility in 2010 every Tuesday evening. Our second facility was Bennington Glen in Marengo, Ohio where we visited once a month and ended with Rufus passing in 2011.

After missing these visits with Rufus, I was referred to a breeder in Mt. Gilead, Ohio who raises Golden Doodles. I found Max in May 2011 and brought him home on Memorial Day. We started training immediately with our trainer in Westerville, Ohio. Max completed both basic and advanced obedience training, earning his Good Citizenship with the AKC. Max started visiting our facilities that we already were approved for.

I was so excited when I was notified by Jan that Max was eligible for recognition for completing 400 hours of visiting patients. Max received his AKC Distinguished Therapy Dog Award on February 19, 2020. In 2021, Max crossed over the Rainbow Bridge.

We are now happy to have Andy, and we are visiting every other week at Woodside Village in Mt. Gilead, Ohio.

Since joining Paws, we have had several therapy dogs: Rufus - 2004-2011; Max - 2011-2021; Sheba - 2015 - 2018; and now, Andy.

Jack and Ruby Linthwaite, Ohio, Paws Members

BINDI, ASA, OLIVER, AND TANGO

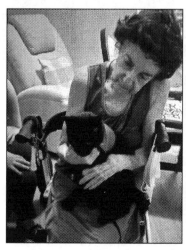 

Approximately five years ago I was leaving my neighborhood when I saw a van covered in paw prints in the lane next to mine. I noticed the name was Paws for Friendship and had pictures of dogs all over it. I saw it parked in a driveway in the neighborhood a few days later. I stopped and spoke to Jan. That was the beginning of a great friendship.

Bindi: My husband and I adopted Bindi (white with red brindle patches) from Greyhound Pets of America Tampa Bay chapter when she was only 16 months old. She was a sweetheart from day one. Whenever I walked her I noticed that she whined when she saw a person. I thought it was just excitement, but I soon learned that that was her way of telling me that she HAD to go and meet that person. To this day, she still whines when she wants to go say "Hi" to anyone. She is a big hit wherever she goes because of her super gentle nature and the fact that she "smiles from both ends." She has a big grin on her face and wags like crazy when she meets someone, old or new. The kids at the elementary school have proclaimed her "the cuddliest dog ever". They hug her, lie all over her, use her for a pillow and even a foot stool while they read to her. She usually falls asleep.

Asa: We adopted Asa (red brindle), whom Bindi chose, from the same organization when she was 2 and had had a very successful racing career. Her career ended when she sustained a tarsal fracture of her right hind leg(the most common injury for greyhounds as they push off with that leg as they round the corners on the track). After giving her several months to adjust to a home life, and exposing her to the big wide world with lots of people, she began her therapy career with Bindi as her mentor.

As it turns out, Asa is somewhat of an empath. She is very friendly, but seems to select those individuals, especially the youngsters, who need her the most. She will stay with them for a while, leave, but often will go back to them later and stay with them. (I have no background info on any of the students prior to the dogs' visits, but sometimes the social worker or guidance counselor will especially note the students' and the dogs' behavior with them and then tell me how pleased they are to see progress on the child's part after the visit.) I have seen students who are non-verbal "converse" with the dogs; non-readers try to read to them; students who are diagnosed as ADHD sit quietly with the dogs, petting them; students who are terrified of dogs, want to hold the leash and pet the dogs after 20 minutes of their gentleness; the list goes on.

Oliver: A black kitten who wandered across my front lawn on one of the hottest days of the year. I scooped him up, placed him inside on my living room sofa and from then on, Oliver ruled. He really liked it when someone came to do some work in my house. From repairmen to installers, Oliver kept them company through the entire job. He especially liked it when someone had a toolbox. Jackpot!! Jan said with his outgoing personality he was potentially useful as a therapy kitty. He was gentle with strangers, put up with kid nonsense and was especially a hit with assisted living folks who missed their kitties or were not particularly "dog people." He loves riding in his stroller or rolling along in his TSA approved carrier. Residents and students love his soft fur, his purring and his gentle nature.

Tango: I already had 2 horses when I took a friend to meet a horse trainer friend of mine. One of the horses I had was not really a good match for me so my trainer friend said, "This is what you need" and proceeded to show me Tango (registered name Cee Gee's Pretty Boy – Spotted Saddle Horse). She said he was a true sweetheart who needed his own person. It didn't hurt that he was drop dead gorgeous; black and white spotted with a flowing mane and white tail. He had been used by her young students and was very gentle. He was also very bright as I found out when I began to expand his training. With his gentle nature, love of kids, and not afraid of challenges he became one of Paws for Friendship's larger therapy animals. Wheelchairs, walkers, and canes don't faze him and he will roll his ball toward someone and they can roll it back to him. We are working on his bow and a few other goodies. Because he is a full-size equine, his visits are all outside the facilities we visit. He is very accepting of wherever I take him and displays very good manners. On one of his visits a child with ADHD actually stood still long enough to hold him and pet him.

Marilyn Griffin, Florida, Paws Member

TABASCO

I joined Paws For Friendship initially with a very social Olde Bulldog named Chomp that my husband and I had rescued. Chomp and I had a wonderful time listening to the kids read at the local library, representing PFF at events, and visiting hospitals and nursing homes. I called it our trifecta of happiness as Chomp and I, and whomever we met that day, were always feeling fantastic by the time we got back to the car. A few years later, I decided to purchase a hatchling Redfoot Tortoise (Tabasco) from a local breeder. I was volunteering with the Clearwater Marine Aquarium at the time and would take the hatchling with me to my aquarium shift where I would share her with staff, volunteers, and visitors. She was a wonderful education tool to learn about the differences between sea turtles and land tortoises and responded positively to the petting and attention. Not long after, I was telling Jan about Tabasco's adventures at the aquarium and jokingly said that she would be a good therapy pet. Jan agreed and Tabasco became a new member right away. Tabasco excels at representing PFF at events and always draws a crowd where she easily connects and enchants people young and old.

Sue Dauterman, Florida, Paws Member

JOY, BOBBY SOCKS, AND PIPER

Like so many members who have submitted personal stories for this special book, I am sure we could all go on and on about the memories we have helped to create and the touching moments that have forever changed our lives. This is a snippet of my journey with Paws for Friendship.

While I was working as a professor at Vincennes University in Indiana, I started looking toward an early retirement with the goal of doing disaster mission work. Many dogs through many years have always been a part of my life, and God just laid it on my heart one day that I should join an organization where I could utilize my babies as therapy pets to accompany me on my missions. I found Paws for Friendship and joined in 2012. I, too, have had several pet members who have crossed the Rainbow Bridge: Tino, Blackjack, Ivy, and Heidi were all members of Paws at one point. They all brought so much enjoyment to the residents we visited at Miller's Merry Manor (now The Waters), in Sullivan, Indiana.

Now, that mission belongs to Piper and Bobby Socks (both Maltese-Yorkie mix) and Joy (a Pomeranian/Poodle/Yorkie mix). There is nothing more rewarding than seeing a smile on a lonely face, a hand reaching to pet a furry bundle of love, a vocal expression of delight when we arrive at the facility. It is a sad reality that these may be the only visits that some residents receive.

So on those Sundays when we visit, and I've come home from church and maybe rue the rigmarole of packing up the "kids" and heading back out, the reward after the fact is ALWAYS a blessing beyond words. Every time – an encounter that is meant to be, a smile at just the right time, a "thank you for coming" melts my heart.

A recent encounter which really moved me was when we walked past a resident's room where he was lying on his bed in semi-darkness and appeared to be sleeping. So we didn't stop. But by the time we came back down the hallway, he had gotten out of bed, was standing in the doorway, and he said he wanted to see the dogs. The amazing thing about the encounter, though, was that this man is almost blind and he cannot really see the dogs. He said he could "see" them with his hands, and he lovingly petted each one.

My dogs have accompanied me on a few mission trip deployments, and have been a comfort to those they encountered. We were in Baton Rouge, Louisiana in 2016 after severe flooding happened there. One of our assignments was to hand out disinfectant spray to combat mold. I had my babies in my truck in the parking lot where we were stationed and people would come over and love on them, tell me their stories, and maybe allow me to pray for them. It was a very touching experience.

That trip led to another very similar one - but for a longer period of time. In 2021, after the devastating flooding in Waverly, Tennessee, we were privileged to be deployed there with an organization I volunteer with, Christ in Action (CIA). I was asked to go in my capacity as a Chaplain with CIA and although dogs normally cannot go on work deployments, this was a unique situation and I was going to be there for a couple of weeks, meeting persons affected by the flood at a volunteer center. And I was approved to bring my dogs with me for the two-week duration.

So I loaded up my camper and we headed south. Ivy (who I still had at that time), Piper, and Bobby Socks provided an intervention and diversion for so many people who were still reeling from the tragedy of the flood and the loss of loved ones. The whole experience was almost indescribable, but I truly felt like I was on a mission for God with my fur babies. Since that first trip, I returned to Waverly five more times - with Piper, Bobby Socks, and now, Joy. The stories of the flood, the friendships I have made, the lives touched because of my babies - they have all had a profound, lasting effect on me, and I am forever grateful to be a part of this amazing organization.

Dottie Stanfill, Indiana, Paws Member

RUGER AND RHIANNA

We started looking to do volunteer work when we were thinking about retiring. We tried out a few things but found doing therapy work and sharing our dogs was the best fit for us. This area of volunteering gave us flexible hours and lots of smiles – from both us and from the people we have visited over the last 15+ years. During our time with Paws we have had six therapy dogs. We have gone to many different types of facilities – from the VA, schools, rehab, hospice, skilled nursing, and assisted living – to public events like memorials, funerals and parades.

We have had the opportunity to make a veteran smile for the last time before he passed away. We have brought comfort to families while their loved one was ill. We create the opportunity for people in memory care to talk about the pets they had growing up and when their kids were growing up. They don't remember the visiting dogs' names, but they respond with pets and hugs. Some people talk to the dogs, though they haven't spoken to family or a caregiver ever. The dogs have helped new residents adjust to their surroundings in both assisted and memory care. The staff at the facilities enjoy the dogs as much as the patients and residents. Staff have reported that after our visits people are more calm, cheerful and they sleep better. They need fewer pain meds or sleeping aids. It is a win for everyone. We have worked with schools during stress week (testing) and helped students who were anxious to be more calm and we have helped them be able to focus on their work.

Every visit is a new experience (though in memory care we hear the same stories every visit). We go from making ambulatory assisted living residents smile to helping someone who has just gone through a loss.

Helping others is also good for us. We are now 75 and 82. Getting out of the house, walking more and focusing on others makes the time go faster. Seeing that our visits make others smile and focus on something other than their pain is rewarding and heart-warming. We get lots of "thanks for coming" and "see you in two weeks" from the places we go regularly. Luckily the dogs enjoy it as much as we do so it is a win-win.

Our very favorite memory is one from 2019. The person had been moved into memory care after his wife passed away. He had been non-verbal for the three days he had been there. Rhianna went and sat next to him. After a muzzle on the knee got no reaction she gently put her paw on his knee. After a moment he looked down, saw her, and picked up her paw in his hands. It was the first intentional movement he had made since arriving. He spoke softly to her and then he looked up and smiled. We all nearly cried.

Karen and Roger Crawford, Arizona, Paws Members

IN MEMORIAM

While many pets who have been members of Paws over the past 30 years have crossed over the Rainbow Bridge and are no longer with us, the following tributes were submitted by current members in memory of their beloved pets. May ALL of our well-adored babies who are no longer with us rest in peace, run with joy, and live like someone left the gate open until we are reunited with them someday.

GABBY - RIP - 2016

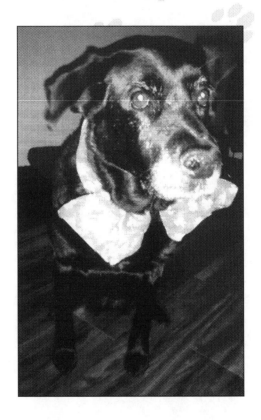

Gabby and I joined Paws for Friendship in 2008. Sadly, Gabby passed away in 2016, and I have not made any visits since. Though I adored taking her to the assisted living facilities where she brought smiles to everyone, my two dogs now do not particularly care to be around anyone but the three humans in our home and one neighbor.

I continue volunteering with Paws because I saw the difference Gabby made in the lives of those living in care centers, as well as the first graders who read to her when I brought her to elementary schools.

Every day I wish my current babies would have the personality to go on visits, but they don't. I don't love them any less. I still serve on the Board, and I help Jan with various tasks and at events when my schedule allows.

Didi Craig, Florida, Paws Member

OLIVIA - RIP 2-15-19

We have known Jan for approximately thirteen years, and we met because of our interest in Paws for Friendship. Jan has always been a kind–hearted soul, who not only loves her members, but all of our fur babies just the same. Her passion for the cause is something you do not often see.

When I brought Olivia's ashes to an event with her vest wrapped around the box of ashes, Jan cried. She is emotionally involved in her cause and friendships. When people are not genuine as she is, she finds it hard to understand why or how people can be this way, and she is hurt deeply. Her passion is what makes everything worthwhile. Those with little passion for anything often misunderstand her.

Jan has been a wonderful friend and leader for Paws for Friendship. We enjoy visiting her when we are in her area. She is always in high spirits and has tons of energy. We can't wait to restart our mission with Paws again!!

Deborah and Steve Hiuchanyk, Florida, Paws Members

SASHA - RIP 11-9-20

After I retired in 2012, I decided I needed some company at home and specifically wanted to rescue a dog. Therefore I began the process of searching for dogs in need of a home, starting with the local county shelter and drove to town to inquire as to what animals were available. My preference was an older, mid-sized dog, preferably part Labrador, and I also wanted a black female (as I once read that black dogs are usually the last to be adopted because people tend to be afraid of them). I didn't see one that filled my expectation, so I went back home and began searching online within a 50 mile radius, only to my surprise there was a five-year old female, black Lab mix, named Sasha, at the very place I had just visited. So I went back to meet her as she had been outside in the exercise yard, and within a few minutes of visiting her, I knew she was perfect for me, so I filled out some paperwork and took her home.

Because my house is in the country, and there are a lot of wild critters running around, I decided we needed to fence in our yard. Upon completion of the installation of the fence, the wife of the business owner stopped over, and I realized I knew her from years ago. There she met Sasha, the newest addition to my family, and I met her canine family. She commented on how mild-mannered Sasha was and thought she might be a great therapy dog and invited me to bring her to a visiting opportunity in connection with the Paws for Friendship organization to which she was a current member.

That very next week, we accompanied my friend and her dogs to two assisted care facilities. Sasha simply walked from room to room and would turn and sit down on the floor next to the resident who was either in a chair or a bed. I sent pictures to Jan at Paws for Friendship and said I was interested in joining her group, as I could see in the faces of those residents the value Sasha brought.

Jan sent me all the paperwork, and we happily signed on! After several visits, Jan arranged for a vest to be made to fit Sasha. That was approximately six months after I had adopted her (or she adopted me; not completely sure which), that we began our journey together with Paws.

Sasha and I visited both assisted care facilities with my friend and her dogs for several months. Then after seeing postings on the Paws website of other animals contributing their time at a public library, I approached the local library and inquired about bringing Sasha there to help children learn to read. The head of the Children's Room asked for a recommendation from one of the assisted care facilities, which was happily granted and submitted. Then Sasha and I met the entire staff of the Children's Room at the library, and they all wholeheartedly agreed that Sasha would be a good fit.

Our volunteer visiting day was always Thursdays – twice monthly we would go to the assisted care facilities and the other two Thursdays we would visit the library. Later on I was approached by 2 separate Christian Schools in the area to give a presentation about pet care and training. After completing those special requests, the library asked for Sasha to come visit specifically the week before the local high school's midterm and final exam dates as she could help de-stress the students while they prepared for their exams. Sasha did a great job – she simply walked among the students who were studying at the tables and waited to be hugged and petted.

Up until the pandemic lockdown in March 2020, Sasha had logged many, many volunteer hours and was recognized by the AKC Registered Therapy Dog organization. She was just shy of a few volunteer hours of the highest honor within the AKC volunteer recognition program – as an "AKC Distinguished Therapy Dog". That following November, on a beautiful autumn day, Sasha crossed over the Rainbow Bridge where she will run and play while no longer in pain.

It was an amazing opportunity for Sasha and me to help others by visiting those in need. As I've said many times, Sasha is the one who did all the work; I was just the driver to take her where she needed to be. Now I ask you . . . Who saved Who?

Karen Slack, Michigan, Paws Member

ROXY - RIP - 2023

Roxy was a little English Bulldog with a heart bigger than she was. She loved visiting with everyone, but her special place was Shriners Hospital. She loved being around the kids. She had some hip problems, so the staff fashioned a special mobility scooter making it easier for her to get around. And making the rounds is exactly what she was determined to do.

The children could see that she also had mobility problems, so they loved her even more. She was determined to visit with every child and show them a disability did not stop her. A disability did not have to stop them either. She gave many the inspiration to try that much harder. Her Mom was told that most of the children weren't progressing with their prosthetic devices. Primarily out of fear. When Roxy was there the children could walk her which in turn enhanced their therapy. She made her way into several rooms where the children were not able to walk around. Everyone absolutely loved her in the 4 years she made her visits. She will dearly be missed, and we extend our sincere sympathy to her Mom. She leaves a wonderful legacy for all to cherish. Roxy helped so many children that were afraid to try their new prosthetics. That has made a tremendous difference those kids will never forget. She had shown them what determination and courage could do. They just had to follow her lead.

(Some excerpts from Sheri Williams on Roxy's Shriners Hospital visits)

Visit notes – Roxy has been able to see many of the same patients for weeks in a row! She has helped a ton with physical therapy. The patients will WORK FOR ROXY, when they won't work for anyone else! We have witnessed remarkable breakthroughs this month, with improvements in physical abilities for patients that have extreme disabilities!

SPECIAL EVENTS THAT TOOK PLACE: Visit Notes 7-6-22 - There was a 5-year-old girl that spent a great deal of time with Roxy that day, while waiting to get her cast off. We went our separate ways, and then a child life specialist yelled to me from down the hall, that she needed me immediately. I found out that the little girl refused to have the staff take the pins out of her arm after they took off the cast. They did everything possible trying to get the pins taken out. Finally, the ONLY thing that changed the girl's mind was hearing the staff say that they would find Roxy, and she would be able to spend time with Roxy after! Once the little girl found out she got to see Roxy again, she stopped fighting the staff, and immediately let them remove the pins from her arm! The Child Life Specialist had promised the little girl that she could see Roxy, and didn't even know if we were still there. She was THRILLED when she saw us, so she could keep her promise to the little girl! We spent more time with the sweet little girl. It was the day that Roxy was not walking well. Roxy was in a wagon. The little girl saw Roxy and climbed right in with her! The staff and mother of the child told me that Roxy was an absolute Godsend, and they did not know what they were going to do if we were not there that day! The mother texted me later that evening and once again told me how thankful she was that Roxy was there today. She said her little girl has not stopped talking about Roxy!

Visit Notes 7-22-22 - Roxy has been working with a young boy for many weeks. When we met Bob at week one, Bob was very scared of Roxy. After watching Roxy do tricks for others, and then for Bob, they have become the best of friends. Bob always has to see Roxy when he is at therapy. Bob loves to watch Roxy ring the bell, do her tricks, and play the piano! Bob even tosses her treats, and she catches the food in the air! This just makes him laugh! On our last visit, Bob refused to do his physical therapy. He was giving the physical therapist an exceptionally hard time, and was not willing to do the proper techniques. So, the physical therapist said, "You cannot see Roxy if you don't do this now!" Bob continued to give them a hard time, so the physical therapist told me to get my bag and Roxy and leave. I stood up to go out the door, when I saw Bob desperately trying to do the proper technique! He yelled, "Wait Roxy, Wait!" He immediately did the proper technique that the physical therapists were asking! He got to see Roxy, and everyone was so proud of him!

Sheri Williams, Louisiana, Paws Member

TICKET - RIP - 2023

"Due to Ticket's jack-of-all-trades therapeutic reputation, she was requested to assist with a teen who was a severe cutter."

My heart is still grieving that I have lost my little Ticket, a one-of-a-kind Border Terrier. Border Terriers can often be found serving as therapy animals in hospitals, schools, and a variety of outpatient and residential settings. A less common type of work where they shine is that of the victim witness-advocacy dog. By nature, Border Terriers are good-tempered, affectionate, obedient, and easily trained. These traits, coupled with Ticket's ability to connect with humans, made her an ideal courtroom dog. I am a practicing defense attorney and I raise Border Terriers. Ticket's great-great-granddaughter, Mynx, is following in Ticket's footsteps with courtroom and therapy visits with Paws for Friendship.

Due to Ticket's jack-of-all trades therapeutic reputation, she was requested to assist with a teen girl who was a severe cutter and nonverbal. The girl was in a locked-down juvenile facility, and all efforts by counselors to engage her in discussion had failed. She had drawn a dog during an art therapy session, so the professionals thought it would be worth a shot to see if she responded to a dog. I was contacted, so I drove Ticket to the facility, and we had to part ways when we reached the last security checkpoint. Ticket walked on with the social worker and never looked back. I was told later that, after hugging Ticket for a very long time, the girl seemed to have a calm descend over her. She wasn't jittery or as withdrawn. She relaxed enough to draw a picture for Ticket. And then she spoke. After months of silence, she said, "Thank you for coming to see me, Ticket."

(This story and more about Ticket can be found in the December 2020 issue of the AKC Gazette).

Ticket developed a brain tumor and made her last therapy visit in the latter part of 2020. It was with a special needs adult at a doctor's appointment. The woman was scared and needed an exam and procedure, and Ticket was a trouper in calming the woman's fears.

Ticket has now crossed over the Rainbow Bridge, but the lives she has touched and the legacy she leaves will always remain in my heart. Seeing the profound impact your dog can have for a human who is suffering is something you will never forget.

D'Arcy Downs-Vollbracht, Arizona, Paws Member

PART III

ALL ABOUT PAWS

HISTORY

- 1993 – Paws for Friendship was founded in Omaha, Nebraska
- 1995 – The organization became incorporated and took on the new title, "Paws for Friendship Inc."
- 1999 – Paws for Friendship Inc. established its status as a 501C3 non-profit organization
- 2006 – International Headquarters relocated from Omaha, Nebraska to Tampa, Florida
- 2023 – Celebrating 30 years of volunteer service to communities across the United States and Canada

Our Website:
www.pawsforfriendshipinc.org

Our Facebook Page:
www.facebook.com/pawsforfriendshipinc

Our Instagram Account:
https://www.instagram.com/paws_for_friendship/

OUR INITIATIVES

- The #1 priority for Paws for Friendship Inc. is visiting those in nursing homes, hospitals, and assisted living centers.
- Our Community Outreach Program provides visits to schools, libraries, adolescent facilities, etc., with our certified therapy pets. These services help children learn better reading skills with our pets as they relax and read to them.
- The Paws on Campus Initiative allows college students access to therapy pets during finals in order to help them cope with stress.
- Organizations such as Kiwanis, SERTOMA, and The Lions have asked for speakers and visits from Paws for Friendship Inc. volunteers.
- Working with Crisis Response Teams to provide therapy pets to those affected by tragedy.

(These are just a few of the programs offered by Paws for Friendship Inc. For additional information, please contact us!)

2022 Services of Love

In 2022, Paws for Friendship Inc. had over 500 human members who made 3,948 visits to 288 different places with 173 four-legged members, volunteering for 11,088 hours!!

ALL ABOUT MEMBERSHIP

Requirements to Join: Paws for Friendship Inc. is a common sense, common courtesy, and respect for volunteer organization that provides facility visits with children, the elderly, and veterans. We expect our members to use common sense and feel they do not need to be told how to act in public. Please know that we do NOT require a Canine Good Citizen (CGC) to join, nor do we encourage "Therapy Dog Classes." We believe in basic obedience, a healthy and well-socialized pet with a loving disposition, common sense, common courtesy, and the desire to truly make a difference in so many lives. These are the *fundamental requirements* needed to join.

Evaluation: Regarding information concerning evaluation requirements – we cannot publish them on our website, but would like to reiterate the need for basic obedience, socialization and a loving disposition. Please be aware, not every pet wants to do this or CAN do this. There are pets that will not pass our evaluation requirements. The pet will always be our number one priority and we ask that you please respect your pet! There are many ways to help in your community if you are unable to do Pet Therapy. We thank you for understanding!

Insurance: Our members are insured, registered, and certified, and we do NOT charge for evaluations of your pet. We have extensive insurance on our members and know that many other groups do not. Please know that the safety of our members and of our two or four-footed friends is our top priority.

New Members: We are grateful you are interested in joining Paws for Friendship Inc. and we will answer any questions you may have. You will be surprised at the difference your pet will make. Sharing your well-adored, well-socialized, well-behaved, and healthy pet can mean the world to someone in a facility who has no family nor friends to visit them. You and your pet can bring joy and happiness to a great many people that otherwise would have none. You will also be surprised at how much your life will be enriched. The value of that, alone, cannot be measured in dollars and cents. It is completely heartfelt and absolutely invaluable.

WHERE WE SERVE

Paws for Friendship members are currently involved in providing volunteer services in the following types of facilities and areas in the states listed:

Assisted Living Facilities in Nebraska, Illinois, Florida, Indiana, New York, Arizona, Connecticut, Massachusetts, Louisiana, Iowa, Mississippi, and Ohio.

Libraries in Iowa, Nebraska, Louisiana, Florida, New York, Indiana, South Dakota, and Texas.

Civic Events in South Carolina, Florida, Massachusetts, New York, Iowa, Arizona, California, and Nebraska.

Medical Facilities in Connecticut, Florida, Nebraska, Indiana, New York, South Carolina, Arizona, and Louisiana.

Schools in Kansas, Indiana, Connecticut, Florida, New York, Massachusetts, Illinois, Iowa, Arizona, Nebraska, Mississippi, Utah, Georgia, California, and Kentucky.

Special Needs in South Carolina, Nebraska, Florida, and Tennessee.

Community Outreach Program:

Our organization provides all services to communities completely free of charge. Here are just a few of the programs in our Community Outreach Program:

- Humane education for the public. We promote diversity and our program has reflected that since we were founded in 1993.
- Paws to Read Programs to promote literacy in schools and libraries from an elementary level to the high school level. We include all grade levels.
- Paws on Campus Program to promote stress relief for students at the high school and college level. Most high schools and colleges have service-learning offices.
- Animal rescue and adoption assistance, subject to member's choice.
- Participation in community events, outreach programs and education forums. We encourage people of all sexual and gender identities, LGBTQ support, racial backgrounds, national origins, abilities, disabilities, religions, ages, etc. to make positive impacts in their community.
- Since we began, we have always visited Veterans facilities, from VA Hospitals to smaller Veterans facilities. Many smiles on their faces tell us our visits are important.
- Speakers for various clubs such as Sertoma Club, Rotary Club, etc. to bring awareness for our program is always welcomed.
- Introducing our program into Critical Care Facilities, such as Dialysis Units, Heart Institutes, Cancer Centers, etc.
- Our focus is to provide friendly interaction between animals and people with the utmost respect. Therapy with animals lowers blood pressure, improves cardiovascular health, releases endorphins that have a calming effect, diminishing overall physical pain; the act of petting produces an automatic relaxation response.

- Our programs are custom to us, copyrighted and trademarked for protection and vary in need to a variety of facilities.
- Our program works with many organizations such as the Give Kids the World Village, Ronald McDonald House, Camp Easter Seals, Special Olympics, etc. Sharing our registered, certified, and insured pets is a privilege we never forget.
- Infection Control policy guidelines are written into our program to allow entrance into hospitals and critical care facilities. All critical care facilities are given copies before our visits begin. We are grateful to comply, so our pets are allowed to visit.
- Paws For Friendship Incorporated is operated solely on donations.

Paws For Friendship Inc. (™)
PO Box 341378 ~ Tampa, Florida 33694
We Are A Non-Profit 501c3 Tax Deductible Volunteer Organization
Email jenniesmom1@gmail.com Web: www.pawsforfriendshipinc.
org **Helping Those In Need One Paw At A Time**
We Are an International Certified Animal Assisted Therapy
Organization
Office (866) 925-PAWS (7297) FL / Cell (813) 957-6829
Fax (866) 728-4828

CELEBRATING 30 YEARS IN 2023

We have been incredibly blessed throughout these 30 years of Volunteer Service to those in need. Our Members understand the commitment of giving back to their communities. Their determination to make the visits to those in need in these tough economic times is challenging at best, but they are committed to making a difference. God has truly blessed us to welcome so many who share in our mission.

Headquarters was relocated to Tampa, FL from Omaha, NE where it remains today. Our growth has been wonderful, and each day brings new adventures for us. Facilities contact us from all over the world and inquire about having our program at their facility. We are constantly looking for people and their loving pets to help us visit those in need. We have been mentioned in many articles concerning the benefits of pet therapy to feeding the 'raw diet' to pets. Our belief is the owner and pet's veterinarian knows your pet better than we do. We stress education and communication between the owner and the veterinarian; this always results in a happy, well loved and cared for pet.

Each time a person joins it signifies their desire to make a difference. Our program allows them to make a difference with their beloved pet. Doors open that were once closed to pet therapy. Critical care areas now welcome the pets because they know the difference they make in people's lives. Someone recovering from surgery or a long-term resident in a care facility can benefit from having the pets visit and share their unconditional love.

Every year we gain new members through a variety of ways. The Internet and Facebook have been invaluable in reaching those miles away. Many have attended an event where we were present, liked our program, believed in our mission, and joined. Our chapters share our mission with those in need. From visiting hospitals to visiting assisted living facilities, hospice, etc. our members share their loving pets with those in need. Our chapters visit facilities ranging from physically and emotionally abused kids, nursing homes to the state veterans homes. We also touch many lives through our Community Outreach Program that encompasses school and library programs; Paws To Read has been incredibly successful and is growing daily.

Our growth has been phenomenal, and each year offers going a little further into new areas such as Crisis Response Teams. Many of our members gave support in Orlando with the nightclub tragedy. Some of our members gave support with the tragedy at Sandy Hook Elementary School in Connecticut.

Determination to make a difference has grown from our foundation in Omaha, Nebraska to where we are today. Overcoming hurdles once placed on keeping an animal out have seen many changes throughout our history. Our members embrace the opportunity to share their pets with so many in need. Too often family members walk away after placing a 'loved one' in a facility. Many times the only interaction residents and patients have is with the paid staff of the facility.

Sharing your registered, insured, and certified pets with those in need of companionship will bring new purpose into your life. That pet you have adored and depended on when you needed comfort in your life will now bring unconditional love to perfect strangers. In a blink of time friendships develop and soon you will realize you brought every wonderful memory of their pets back into their lives. Every cherished memory will be remembered and shared with you because you cared enough to visit with them. They adore your pets, and they are grateful you took the time from your busy schedule to bring your little angel to visit with them.

All tax-deductible donations received go toward operating costs such as copies, mailings, office supplies, membership materials, insurance and other costs involved in running the organization. We are all volunteers. Donations completely support us to operate and grow. All monies and donations are used for the entire organization, regardless of location. Fundraising efforts go a tremendous way in increasing the number of volunteers who will be able to serve the facilities that have requested our services. Many volunteers average one hour of volunteer service per week while many make several visits per month. We realize how busy everyone is and our visits are to be enjoyed by all, not to cause added stress in anyone's life. Many volunteers visit multiple facilities each week. The need for caring and compassion, especially accompanied by a wagging tail, will never end. In reaching out to others, our lives are enriched beyond definition. This is something that cannot be measured in dollars and cents; it is much more valuable than that. It is a legacy you will leave for others to help them leave theirs. To make a difference in someone's life is wonderful, far beyond measure, and it truly "takes a village."

Thirty years ago, our beloved Founder, Jennie, walked into a care center not knowing what to expect. She took me along with her because she knew something well before I did. The look from her after she approached a woman in a wheelchair and placed her head in her lap told me everything. This woman kissed her, hugged, and petted her as if old friends. Jennie looked at me as if to say, "Be my voice and I will be your strength." I was, and she is, and her legacy continues to make a difference to this very day. Her heart and soul embrace every member all around the world. Her legacy will span generations because of her determination to show unconditional love for everyone regardless of illness, disability, or injury.

Paws For Friendship Incorporated began with Jennie. She alone began a journey that would bring many lives together and enrich them beyond measure. I was blessed to share 11 ½ years with this angel. I continue every day to live her legacy with immense pride.

Sincerely,
Jennie's Mom, Jan

Time to Live...........

Life grants us the opportunity to write our own destiny. Our fate is not a matter of chance; it is how we decide to spend our lives. Let us choose to give our lives to something that will outlast us.

ABOUT THE AUTHOR

Usually, it's a human who rescues a dog or a cat or some other pet that experienced a traumatic life. Jan Schmidt shares her unlikely story of being rescued herself by a little Great Dane named Jennie. Jan was struggling with despair and depression following the death of her mother. She was contemplating suicide at one point when, through what she calls "divine intervention", she met Jennie who was six months old at the time. Abused and neglected and close to being "put down", Jan took Jennie home, and they began a bond that laid the groundwork for touching thousands of lives. Jan often thought about the residents at the care center where her mom had been - those lonely individuals who waited patiently for someone who never would arrive—a family member, a former neighbor, anyone. So one day, she took Jennie and they drove to the facility.

"I suddenly felt a wave of terror and knew I could not do this— after all those years and all those lonesome faces. I began to turn away just inches from that first mat and headed towards the van. Suddenly, Jennie pulled me back around and literally forced me inside. I wanted to run away but Jennie knew we had to stay."

And so began the very first visit and the birth of Paws for Friendship, Incorporated - the journey of Jennie, a little Great Dane, and her "designated driver", Jan.

Printed in the United States
by Baker & Taylor Publisher Services